LOS ANGELES

IN THE

THIRTIES

1931 - 1941

California Architecture and Architects, Number 7
David Gebhard, Editor

1.   Downtown Los Angeles
     c. 1939

LOS ANGELES
IN THE
THIRTIES

1931 - 1941

Second Edition
Revised and Enlarged

DAVID GEBHARD
AND
HARRIETTE VON BRETON

Hennessey + Ingalls   Santa Monica

Published by
Hennessey + Ingalls
214 Wilshire Boulevard
Santa Monica CA 90401

www.hennesseyingalls.com

First published by Hennessey + Ingalls, 1975
Second, revised and enlarged edition, published in 1989
Reprinted, 2006

13 digit ISBN: 978-0-912158-97-6
10 digit ISBN: 0-912158-97-2

Library of Congress Cataloging-in-Publication Data

Gebhard, David.
    Los Angeles in the thirties, 1931-1941 / David Gebhard and
  Harriette Von Breton. – 2nd ed., rev. and enlarged.
      p.   cm.   -- (California architecture and architects ; no. 7)
    Rev. ed. of L.A. in the thirties, 1931-1941.
    Includes index.
    Bibliography: p.
    ISBN 0-912158-97-2 (pbk.)
1. Architecture—California—Los Angeles. 2. Architecture, Modern—20th
  century—California—Los Angeles. 3. Los Angeles (Calif.)—Buildings, structures, etc. I. Von Breton, Harriette. II. Gebhard, David. L.A. in the thirties,
1931-1941. III. Title. IV. Series.
NA735.L55G42   1989
720' .9794'94—dc19   89-1973

Front cover: Sunset Tower Hotel; Leland Bryant, 1929-31
Back cover: Griffith Park Observatory; John Austin & F. M. Ashley, 1935
Photographs courtesy of Tim Street-Porter

CONTENTS

ACKNOWLEDGMENTS

This publication grew out of an exhibition entitled *L.A. in the Thirties* presented at the Art Galleries of the University of California, Santa Barbara, between April 8th and May 11th, 1975. As with any exhibition and publication, numerous individuals, businesses, and public bodies have contributed in a substantial way. Among these the authors would especially like to thank the following: Gregory Ain; Robert Alexander; John Beach; David Bricker; Lauren Weiss Bricker; John Chase; Roland Coate, Jr.; The Farmer's Market, Los Angeles; First Federal Savings of Hollywood; Ralph C. Flewelling, Sr.; General Telephone Co. of California, Los Angeles; Harwell Hamilton Harris; Alan Hess; Joseph Johnson; A. Quincy Jones; H. Roy Kelley; Maria Kipp; Paul Laszlo; S. Charles Lee; Richard Longstreth; Los Angeles (City), Department of Planning, Los Angeles; Los Angeles County, Department of Regional Planning, Los Angeles; Los Angeles County Museum of Natural History, History Division, Los Angeles; Max Factor, Inc., Hollywood; Esther McCoy; Raymond McKelvey; National Broadcasting Corp., Los Angeles; Wallace Neff; Dione Neutra; Thomas Owen; Pasadena Public Library, Pasadena; Pacific Telephone Co., Santa Monica; Herbert J. Powell; Marvin Rand; George Vernon Russell; Pauline Schindler; Mel Scott; Julius Shulman; Raphael Soriano; Southern California Chapter, American Institute of Architects, Los Angeles; Mary Swafford; Department of Transportation, State of California, Los Angeles; University of California, Los Angeles, Special Collections, Los Angeles; Ellen Vanderlip; Robert Winter; Lloyd Wright.

We also wish to express our appreciation to Sonya Olsen, Sharon Swigart, and Patricia Gebhard for their criticisms and preparation of the original (1975) manuscript. Finally, credit must be given to the following art history graduate students who gathered and presented many stimulating ideas in a seminar on Los Angeles given in the fall of 1974 in the Art Department of the University of California, Santa Barbara: Jane Ann Barthelme, Douglas Ray Ford, Robert G. Ingersoll, Tracey Anne Loeb, Melinda Anne Lorenz, Rebecca E. Love, Roselle Pozomke, Margaret Proskauer, Doran Henry Ross, Barry N. Zarakov.

INTRODUCTION

IF EVER THERE WAS an area set up for an extravaganza, it was Southern California. The extraordinary climate, idyllic beaches and seashore, beautiful mountains and valleys filled promoters and supersalesmen with unquenchable enthusiasm and optimism. Siren songs of riches and paradise filled the air. The space was there, the resources were there, and the spirit was there. The population explosion of the country was magnetically drawn to this glorious Shangri-la by a public relations program that has known few equals for its persistence and volume. Los Angeles and Southern California thrived and prospered on well-cultivated propaganda.

Vital, wayward, greedy, optimistic Los Angeles, gargantuan frontier child of amorphous Southern California, sent out its tentacled arterials to consume deserts and seashores, lovely valleys, orange groves, fields and streams with an ever-increasing appetite. It pushed continuously against seemingly inexhaustible boundaries as jokes were made about road signs pointing to the City Hall 60 miles away. There was no end to the horizon.

Talented professional planners and architects were inevitably attracted to this utopia, where so much was fermenting and so many opportunities lay unexplored. Small wonder that, by the 1930s, the area embraced some of the most innovative, competent, and successful design talent in the world.

Even the real fear of water shortages was solved when the Colorado River Aqueduct spilled its bounties into the thirsty maw of the growing metropolitan area. The San Fernando Valley boomed and blossomed. A giant coliseum was built in Exposition Park to open the Xth Olympiad on July 30, 1932. The Griffith Park Planetarium was dedicated in 1935; and the new Union Passenger Terminal ("the most modern in America"), in 1939. Huge public buildings were dedicated to the future by intrepid leaders, who were guiding the destinies of the area onward, upward, and ever outward.

Frequently called "the newest city in the world," or "the city without a past," Los Angeles embraced all and everything that came to its bounteous bosom. The advent of the Depression did little to cool down this powerful force of ideas, men, space, and resources. It did make a temporary dip in the growth graph, but there was too much going on to really stop the boom, and then, of course, the Los Angeles Chamber of Commerce did not permit such disloyalty.

As a result of the Depression, designs all over the U.S. were simplified from the extravagant '20s, and there was a developing interest in streamlining. Paul T. Frankl wrote in 1930, "Ornament = crime." Good design was an important enrichment for art objects and everyday objects that could be mass produced and made available to all. "Art in Industry," a slogan projected by many manufacturers, was a challenge to use technology to produce beautiful and useful objects and buildings. The obsession was with total design that left no ugly, neglected corners to offend the sensibilities. A new American style flourished.

Architects and designers were challenged and stimulated by a richness of materials, especially glass. Architectural magazines of the period were filled with compelling ads for glass, glass brick, the value of glass walls for light, privacy, and sun worship. Black glass, sand-etched glass, mirrors of all dimensions, shapes,

1

and colors were heralding the age of glass—the new material for Moderne houses and public buildings.

The list of other new materials seemed staggering. Aluminum, cork, Bakelite, Formica, structural mirrors, patent leather, chrome-plated steel, aluminum tube, Monel metal, decorative tiles, silver, gold, and pewter, to name a few, led designers into new forms—round corners, bent tubes, and circles. Dazzled by these most modern materials, leading American architect-designers and artists were anxious to adapt industrial processes to extend their possibilities.

Metals and wood were available for decorative as well as structural use; all were combined or juxtaposed in an enrichment of detail and surface. Design application and ornamentation, form, line, and color were everybody's game. Bas-relief, murals, and sculpture were all being incorporated into architecture and were appearing not only as exterior ornamentation, but in interiors, including much-neglected bathrooms and kitchens. The temptations were irresistible.

Furniture was a major concern, not only of designers, but also of architects, who frequently insisted on designing interiors and built-in furniture for their buildings. Brilliant craftsmen were needed to execute the designs, and the return of the crafts was heralded by writers and editors as a renaissance of creativity in the ideal environment.

In L.A. the new developments flourished in spite of the hypnotic effect of the climate and palm trees. There was a flowering of new forms and designs, a combining of materials in a fresh, spirited way; and public art flourished.

Certainly, one of the most powerful forces influencing design in Southern California was the mobility of the population. Streamlining and the Moderne were perfect expressions for an automobile-oriented society. In an affirmation of faith in the future, the aesthetics of speed, freedom, and mobility were applied to buildings, trains, ocean liners, aircraft, refrigerators, radios—anything. Los Angeles is filled with classic examples of the curved corners and sculptured masses of the Moderne, such as the Academy Theatre by S. Charles Lee, the Pan-Pacific Auditorium by Charles F. Plummer, Walter Wurdeman, and Welton Becket, the McCullough Building by Welton Becket, and the well known Coca-Cola Building by Robert V. Derrah. This drive for freedom, flow, and mobility finally culminated in the design of the Silverstream mobile home, a com-

pletely streamlined package for living on the move. Fanciful drive-in architecture also met the growing demands of a mobile society. The alluring Farmer's Market, a traveling gourmet's delight, opened in 1934.

Art schools flourished during this period. Art Center School, one of the most successful professional training schools in the country, taught photographers, painters, sculptors, and craftsmen of all kinds with a staff of stars such as Ansel Adams, Will Connell, and Kem Weber. Many other schools such as the Otis Art Institute, Chouinard, the colleges and universities—the University of California, Los Angeles, Pepperdine, Occidental, the University of Southern California, the California Institute of Technology, and the Claremont Colleges—drew artists, scholars, and innovative thinkers from all over the globe to create an intellectual community of ideas and experimentation. All of these first-class educational institutions, located within the boundaries of Southern California, had excellent departments of art with teachers who were also activists in stimulating the flow and execution of ideas, the physical expression of new life styles, and the uses of the new technology.

Superb craftsmen such as Otto and Gertrude Natzler, Glen Lukens, and Beatrice Wood in ceramics, and Maria Kipp, Tilli Lorch, Paul Laszlo, and Paul T. Frankl in textiles were becoming eminent in their fields, setting standards of high excellence and productivity. Annual exhibitions by artists in the L.A. vicinity proliferated.

Adding to the circus-drama atmosphere was the giant film industry with its own set of professional designers, producers, promoters, and public relations experts. The extravagances of theatrical architecture influenced many designers. S. Charles Lee, a leading theatre designer, combined Moderne and decorative detail to produce theatres that were loved and admired as pure "Hollywood." Etched aluminum and repoussé were among the metals and materials molded here into fluid forms accented by the color, light, and shadow of neon lighting, which came into full flower in the '30s. The lively, wealthy film industry was searching out new motifs and symbols for pictures of historical context; all of this Los Angeles saw and embraced. Combined, it was a mighty potent brew.

Ever since the California Ranchos became cities, Wilshire Boulevard has veined its way from success to failure to success. Surviving politicians' manipulations, land speculators'

2

exploitation, and even the Depression, it has stretched its way to the Pacific from the heart-zone of the city and has been a symbol of tenacious and spirited growth and development. Reaching ever west it has epitomized the vitality and imaginative thrust of Southern California. Called the "Fifth Avenue of the West" (although it never was), it has been segmented into unique shopping and business areas, and, especially in the '30s, posh residential zones. It has been (and still is) an insinuating piece of the landscape that no one can escape. Other long, varied arterials, such as Sunset Boulevard (a close second to Wilshire), Santa Monica Boulevard, Vermont Avenue, or Ventura Boulevard, never had the focus of concentrated love, hate, and greed—or the starring role—that Wilshire had. Its façade mirrors the remarkable variety of the scene as it winds its way from the downtown district through MacArthur Park, past Bullock's Wilshire and the Ambassador Hotel, through the intersections of Western Avenue and Crenshaw Boulevard to the Miracle Mile, on to La Cienega Boulevard and Beverly Hills, past U.C.L.A., Westwood, and the Veterans Administration Hospital and Cemetery on Sawtelle, then on to Santa Monica and the blue Pacific. What a boulevard! It is practically a 16-mile measuring stick for the growth and exploitation that were to change the Southern California pastoral landscape. Fashions of architectural expression, booms and busts, the rearranging of values and space, as ideas and schemes rooted and flowered, or died—are all reflected on Wilshire.

Film stars Claudette Colbert, Greta Garbo, Douglas Fairbanks, Joan Crawford, William Powell, Myrna Loy, and Robert Taylor all cruised up and down Wilshire Boulevard in their streamlined, often custom-made automobiles, from the city to the sea. The whole mobile society drove its length in compulsive wandering, arriving, and returning. As voguish ideas multiplied, Wilshire became a long showroom of sights, sounds, ideas, and dreams.

To the south and west of Wilshire, on the periphery of Los Angeles, lay the idyllic beach communities of Malibu, Santa Monica, Venice, Manhattan Beach, Hermosa Beach, Redondo Beach, Portuguese Bend, and Palos Verdes. Palos Verdes, for example, was designed as a dazzling planned residential community, a mecca for the nation, by the imaginative and brilliant planners Frederick Olmsted, Jr. and Albert Olmsted, and by architect Myron C. Hunt. Because of the ex-ceptional beauty of the area and the original soundness and character of the planning, it has remained a unique beach-oriented residential area, even though, during the Depression, taxes became delinquent, and until 1937, financing was an impossibility.

To the north and east of Wilshire lay the mountain communities of Pacific Palisades, Brentwood, Bel Air, Beverly Hills, the Hollywood Hills, the Los Feliz Hills, Silverlake and, farther out, Glendale, Eagle Rock, La Cañada, and Flintridge. Parts of these communities were located in foothills, which were intersected by deep, precipitous canyons. The terrain demanded special architectural styles. They emphasized a kind of rural life style close to the boulevards and business communities. Residential designers employed several solutions in order to use these sites. Some designs had framed substructures and supports anchored into the hillsides; others adopted the form of Cliff May's sprawling rural California ranch houses, which were admired and adapted across the country. Breathtaking views and a sense of space, with an illusion of country life and rural quiet, quickly drew a population to these canyons and hillsides and gave architects fresh opportunities for innovative designs.

The old and the new met in the '30s. The new architectural vocabulary that culminated in the New York World's Fair of 1939 had already been formulated and adapted to Southern California. The modern house came into its own; some called it the "California house." However, 90 percent of the architects were still building period architecture. French Norman, Tudor, Spanish, Monterey, Georgian, and Colonial were being erected for rich film and business clients at the same time that Richard J. Neutra and Rudolph Schindler were developing their personal versions of the International Style with dazzling virtuosity. Frank Lloyd Wright and Lloyd Wright were designing humane, original, ingenious residences and issuing warnings against mass housing and the destruction and rape of the environment long before these became popular issues. Ralph C. Flewelling and H. Roy Kelley were designing beautiful, dignified Spanish structures; Roland E. Coate, elegant Georgian and period houses. A. Quincy Jones, Harwell Hamilton Harris, Gregory Ain, and Raphael Soriano, all original, gifted talents, made Southern California a unique and rarified scene of numerous options. Almost anything the heart

3

could possibly desire could be designed and built. The important thing was that good design, regardless of the vocabulary, became the concern of more than a few wealthy elite and was considered a good investment and a part of daily life.

Southern California received its share of contracts under programs of the federal Public Works Administration (P.W.A.), and building and the arts received a simultaneous inoculation of funds. By 1935, productivity soared. Public and private multiple housing, such as Baldwin Hills Village and the Ramona Gardens, was on the drawing boards. Murals and sculptures began to appear in public squares, lobbies of public buildings, libraries, schools, and post offices. The dream of mass production was becoming a reality, and large segments of the public were beginning to recognize, own, and buy good design. Manufacturers and retailers were investing in it because it was sound business practice —it paid off.

The Arroyo Seco Parkway (now the Pasadena Freeway), built in the late '30s, began to suggest the geographical changes that would come to Southern California. Freeways invaded and opened isolated pockets that had seen little growth or change. They penetrated the rural community with a stilettolike violence —altering growth patterns, the landscape, even the climate. The Cahuenga Pass Freeway opened the San Fernando Valley and eventually changed it into

a second metropolis. Fortunately, the sprawling landscape into which freeways did not penetrate maintained much of its original character, but thousands of acres of landscape were irrevocably rearranged.

A focus for all this abundant talent and opportunity was the Los Angeles-based publication *California Arts and Architecture,* whose editor, John Entenza, stimulated innovative design and educated his readers. Ideas, architecture, and crafts were encouraged; in addition, they were uninhibited by concerns of shortages or by lack of space or money. By 1935 the backlog of building and housing erupted like a capped volcano, and a body of work of original architectural spontaneity was achieved. An increasing appetite, and often a gourmet one, prepared for the future feast of the '40s and '50s.

On December 7, 1941, the Japanese attacked Pearl Harbor. Southern California was blacked out, and gas rationing was instituted. Japanese-Americans were forcibly uprooted and taken into custody, and their fishing fleet was quarantined. The productive flow was diverted to weapons, and GIs passed through Los Angeles and Southern California on their way to the Pacific theatres of war. The extravagant dream was temporarily abandoned for the even more extravagant demands of war.

—Harriette Von Breton

4

THE SCENE

URING THE DEPRES-
sion years of the 1930s there was one locale
which, both in myth and in fact, seemed to retain
and even to continue the optimism of former decades. This was the city of Los Angeles, and
specifically, the community of Hollywood. The
Los Angeles scene, as portrayed in films, weekly
radio broadcasts, and the press, seemed to mirror just what most Americans throughout the
country felt their world should be like. The Hollywood version of the "average" middle-class
American family lived in a quiet, suburban setting, in a spacious Colonial Revival house, tastefully furnished in Early American reproductions,
with two or more automobiles in the family garage. Any easy abundance of material goods
was available, ranging from groceries obtained at
the nearest drive-in supermarket to consumer
goods from fashionable suburban specialty and
department stores.

For those caught in the gloom of the Depression, this arcadia was, to be sure, somewhat
hazy and perhaps a bit unreal. But like the
streamlined world of Flash Gordon and Buck
Rogers, there was enough substantial reality
about it to make it plausible. Neither the actual
life style of Los Angeles during this decade, nor
the portrayal of it via films and radio was ever so
farfetched as to alienate the millions of believers
throughout the country who shared the middle-
class dream.

While playing this arcadian role during the
Depression, Los Angeles was not the instigator
of major innovations, but rather a mirror of
middle-class taste. Los Angeles' role from the
mid-19th century to the present has been one of
taking up ideas that have originated elsewhere
and then expanding on them in ways never
conceived of before.

The City of Angels was certainly not the first
U.S. community to build a freeway, to develop
the various forms of drive-in architecture, to
extend the commercial strip, or to pursue the
ideal of a completely decentralized city. But by
the end of the '30s, L.A. was the only city where
all of the essential ingredients of the horizontal,
private-auto-oriented city were firmly established.
Only the outbreak of direct U.S. involvement in
World War II prevented their full realization in
1942 and 1943.

The same pattern also holds true for architecture. L.A.'s architectural productions during
the '30s were impressive for several reasons.
L.A. attracted and held a remarkable array of
architectural talent and an equally impressive
group of prospective clients. Also, there was
money, so buildings continued to be designed
and constructed. While there were highly talented period revival architects practicing in the
East, Midwest, and in the Bay region of California itself, no one locale could, in any way, equal
the refined sophistication of L.A.'s contingent of
period revival architects, which included John
Byers, Roland Coate, Reginald D. Johnson,
Gordon B. Kaufmann, H. Roy Kelley, Edla Muir,
Ralph C. Flewelling, Wallace Neff, George
Vernon Russell, Palmer Sabin, Carleton M.
Winslow, and Paul R. Williams. The work of
these men filled the pages of low- to middle-brow
magazines such as *American Home* and the
more pretentious *House Beautiful, Architectural
Digest,* and *House and Garden.* Their work was
continually featured in the professional architec-
tural journals, *Architectural Forum, Architectural
Record,* and *Pencil Points.*

While there was a smattering of avant-garde
Modern and Streamline Moderne architecture
elsewhere in the country, no area, with the

5

possible exception of San Francisco, was as hospitable to the Modern avant-garde—ranging from the machine precisionism of Richard J. Neutra to the DeStijl forms of R.M. Schindler— as was Los Angeles. Neutra, Schindler, J.R. Davidson, Harwell H. Harris, Gregory Ain, and Raphael Soriano created a corpus of work, which, by 1940, could aptly be referred to as the "Los Angeles School." Also, the city and its environs were a haven for the popular version of the new architecture, the Streamline Moderne, with its white stucco surfaces, curved corners, and glass bricks. No other designer in the country could equal the output and quality of commercial Moderne that came from the L.A. office of Stiles O. Clements. The shopping center, the drive-in supermarket, and the auto-oriented suburban department store were new architectural forms, which he helped to perfect functionally by 1941. Plans by eastern and midwestern designers for suburban motion-picture theatres—in the '30s, one of the few building types that continued to be constructed all over the country—seemed pale in comparison to the hundred plus designs that came from the L.A. office of S. Charles Lee.

2. Wilshire Boulevard,
looking east from
Fairfax Avenue
1930

3. Wilshire Boulevard
   at Western Avenue,
   looking east
   1941

4. Wilshire Boulevard
   at MacArthur Park
   c. 1937

5. Westwood Village
   c. 1930

6. Westwood Village
   1941

7. Santa Monica Beach
   c. 1930

8. Santa Monica Palisades
   1930

9. Malibu
   c. 1939

10

11

12

12

10. San Fernando Valley
    c. 1940

11. Real estate office in Cahuenga
    Park
    San Fernando Valley
    c. 1941

12. Beverly Hills
    1928

13. View over the Hollywood
    Hills north to the San
    Fernando Valley
    1941

14. Hollywood, near Rossmore
    Avenue
    1930

15. Opening at Grauman's Chinese Theatre,
    Hollywood Boulevard
    1937

16. Night scene
    Beverly Hills, c. 1932

17. Downtown Los Angeles at night
    c. 1941

18. Neon sign for the Xth Olympiad
1932

THE PLAN

Los Angeles' gangling growth makes everybody happy, except U.S. city planners. (*Time,* 10 November 1941)

In 1941 THE LOS ANGELES County Regional Planning Commission published *A Comprehensive Report on the Master Plan of Highways for Los Angeles County*—one of the most significant of their numerous reports. It contained what they felt should be the guiding principles for the growth and development of the greater Los Angeles region.

> The Commission, therefore, believes that to conform with actual events and processes it is necessary as well as desirable to provide for future population in this region by encouraging the development of various smaller cities and towns throughout the region, until one reaches an optimum size, rather than by the indiscriminate and unbroken expansion of the central urban area . . . . This region can and should remain one in which the single-family dwelling predominates.[1]

These, then, were the basic principles that were to guide the growth pattern for post-World War II Los Angeles. It was to be a decentralized city with a number of regional hubs. The traditional central business core, downtown L.A., was to be simply one of many commercial centers, and not necessarily even the largest. The private automobile was to be cultivated as the principal mode of transportation. A network of freeways and parkways was to be built to accommodate this prime mode of transportation. The major element, the heart, of the new, decentralized city was not to be industrial complexes, business or governmental centers, but a low-density dispersal of the single, free-standing house.

Obviously, Los Angeles as we know it today was not created—as has often been suggested—by accident, chance, or non-planning. This classic non-city (in a traditional sense) was a planned non-city. With this in mind, the growth and land-use pattern found throughout the L.A. Basin becomes understandable. Without being unduly nostalgic, it is possible to argue that, by 1941, L.A. came about as close as is humanly possible to realizing the American middle-class view of the ideal environment. Suburbia was equated with the overpowering righteousness of nature and the virtue of rural life, while it was widely suspected that the traditional high-density city was, of necessity, evil and corrupt. Though Frank Lloyd Wright, at the time, cast a jaundiced glance at L.A.—"it is as if you tipped the United States up so that all of the common people slid down into Southern California"—the city and its region came remarkably close to mirroring his belief in the auto and the horizontal, decentralized planning of his Broad Acre City.[2]

Los Angeles' ability to realize the ideal of the low-density, horizontal city was the result of a number of closely intertwined elements. The most salient of these were the uniqueness of its geographic and climatic environment, the historic moment when L.A. emerged as a major urban center, the peculiarity of its economic bases (land speculation, oil, the motion-picture industry, aircraft production, tourism), and the open and cultivated hedonism of its middle-middle and upper-middle classes.

L.A. had been a booster's paradise since the 1870s, and the P.R. quotes commonly used to describe it are often so outrageous, so unbelievable, that they are a delight. Early in 1869, for example, Oscar Shuch noted: "Southern California constitutes one vast garden, cut up into a world of Edens. The ecstatic heart spontaneously exalts at the growing magnificence and glories at the prospect of its future existence."[3] Though L.A. in the 19th century went through boom after boom, it was still a small community numbering only 100,000 residents in 1900. But from that time on, the city and its surrounding region began to grow at an incredible pace. By 1920 the city had increased its population five-fold, reaching 576,673. At the end of the speculator-boom days of the 1920s, L.A. at last topped a million, growing to 1,238,048 by 1930. More indicative, though, of what was actually occurring was the increased horizontal spreading of the community. The region, exclusive of L.A., increased from 936,000 to 2,208,000, with the result that, by 1930, the region had double the population of its supposed parent city.[4]

Matching the growth in population was the physical expansion of the city of Los Angeles. Its 1930 area of 442 square miles made it the largest city in the nation, but its real boundaries were not political, for the surrounding communities slowly tended to congeal and form one loose whole. While many individual locales maintained a sense of separateness—Santa Monica, Beverly Hills, Burbank, Pasadena—this sense was only incidentally based on the political independence or nonindependence of the community. Some like San Marino were political as well as social entities; others like Hollywood, Bel Air, or Brentwood were separate in feeling and fact, though politically they were only districts within the city or county.

The downward economic skid of the early '30s slowed L.A.'s growth, at least when compared to the two previous decades. The 1930 population of the city (1,238,048) had risen only 20.9 percent to 1,496,792 in 1940. Once again, though, as had happened in the '20s, the area growth of 25.8 percent—to a total of 2,777,211—surpassed that of the city. These population figures only marginally explain the transformations taking place in L.A. at the time.

What sort of environment were these Angelenos cooking up for themselves? First, it had the lowest density per square mile to be found in any U.S. urban environment. There was nothing to compare with it. Second, the predominant and favored item in that environment was the single, freestanding house. The degree to which L.A. was unique can be sensed by comparing it with Detroit, which also had a low population density compared to other U.S. cities. In 1930, 79.9 percent of Detroit's housing was single-family residential, while in Los Angeles, 93.9 percent was single-family housing. The difference between the two cities became even more marked by 1941, when single-family housing accounted for 39.6 percent of the land use in the Los Angeles urban area.

L.A.'s linear spread over the countryside was made possible by the successful solution of three environmentally related problems: how to provide transportation, how to build the needed economic base, and how to supply water and energy to meet the needs of the expanding population and of industry.

Through World War I, L.A. relied to a degree on the extensive Pacific Electric and its companion Los Angeles Electric for its transportation.[5] The Pacific Electric lines were of two types: urban-street lines used for daily transportation to work and to shop; and longer intercommunity lines, which united the existing communities of the area. The Pacific Electric was not really used by many of its riders as a suburban commuter line such as was found in the East and Midwest. Nor can it be said that the Pacific Electric was influential in establishing the urban dispersion of the Basin. It merely reinforced patterns that already existed. By the end of the teens, Pacific Electric, like most urban transportation systems in the U.S., was in poor financial shape, relying increasingly on direct and indirect governmental support. By 1920 its formidable competitor was the private automobile. In that year there were 160,530 private autos registered in L.A. County; by 1930, 806,264; and by 1940, 1,093,290. In 1941 the Regional Planning Commission (with an evident shedding of tears by some members of its professional staff) noted in its official report, A Master Plan For Highways, that, "As long as adequate streets and highways are provided, the people of the region will not readily abandon the flexible mobility of the individually owned motor car."[6]

The suburban spread of population over much of the Basin meant that, by the beginning of the '30s, industry and business were not, as was traditionally the case, situated within a limited locale at or near the center of the urban core. L.A.'s peculiar geographic arrangement with its business center located approximately twenty miles north of its port facilities at San Pedro and Wilmington was just one early indication that its later expansion was hardly going to follow any older classic pattern. By 1930 its major industries (excluding tourism)—oil, rubber, and the automobile—were already dispersed over a large area; and new patterns were rapidly emerging for retail shopping and office space. Linear development was already a going concern at the western end of the city, with Wilshire Boulevard as its commercial spine.[7] Though a number of office buildings were built in downtown L.A. during the '20s, including the black-and-gold Richfield Building and the green-and-gold Columbia and Eastern Outfitters Building (now the Eastern Columbia Building), the most interesting constructions, from a planning viewpoint, were those built on Wilshire, away from downtown.[8] The elegant Bullock's Wilshire of 1928 was joined by a score or more of low-rise office and commercial buildings. Wilshire's Miracle Mile, officially so named in 1928, was, by the early 1930s, *the place* to have an office and to shop. Other commercial strips were on their way by the end of the 1920s. Parts of Santa Monica, Sunset, and Hollywood Boulevards and Melrose Avenue sprouted a wide variety of commercial buildings, most of which were small, one-story retail stores.

From their beginnings in the '20s, these strips were directly oriented to automobiles, not to pedestrians. Whether L.A. originated the new 20th century forms of drive-in architecture may never be known with historical exactitude, but no one could contest the fact that, by the 1930s, she boasted the largest array of drive-in buildings to be found anywhere in the country. These drive-in structures ranged from Bullock's Wilshire, whose main entrance actually faced the parking lot, to numerous restaurants, and over a dozen drive-in markets, some of which were already small-scale shopping centers.[9] Some, such as El Adobe or the Palm Market, opened in an L-shaped fashion upon their parking space, while others like the Mandacin supplemented the normal run of stores with the addition of a complete automotive service center. Inventiveness abounded: "everything is easily available for the motorist, including a free pony ride for the children."[10]

How did official, formal planning fit itself into this peculiar world of the non-city? A careful reading of the published histories of planning and the planning profession in L.A. gives the distinct impression that the task of the planner was to bureaucratize and codify that which existed. Only in

the planning and design of freeways and in providing for the Basin's water and energy needs did the work of the planners run neck and neck with that of the real world.

Throughout the 20th century, L.A. had been in the vanguard of adopting not only those elements professional planners abhor, but also those they have so dearly felt to be essential to the well-planned, well-ordered community.[11] In 1904 L.A. created its first zoning code, as one would expect of the "lotus land of the south," for the open and avowed purpose of protecting a residential district from any impingement by non-residential activities. Four years later, L.A. was *the first* U.S. city to adopt a comprehensive zoning ordinance that applied to the whole city. In 1910 it established the City Planning Commission, and in 1923 state legislation was sought, and granted, to provide for the Los Angeles County Regional Planning Commission. At the end of the '20s, as a result of considerable pressure from the Los Angeles area, the State Planning Act was passed to provide the mechanism for establishing legal master plans for the cities of California.

All of this has an impressive ring, but in truth much of the legislation and many of the commissions that were established never really ended up functioning in quite the manner supposedly intended for them. As one would expect of L.A., the one and only planning aspect that was in any way carried out had to do with streets and highways for the private car. In 1921 the first *Comprehensive Major Street Plan* was adopted, and this was amplified and expanded in 1931. Great progress was made in the '20s in planning and developing a system of primary and secondary streets and highways.

By 1930 only 48 percent of the city was actually zoned, but then this sort of planning was really marginal to L.A.'s needs. The L.A. view of planning and land use was, in essence, no different from that of the rest of the country. The consensus was that land was a speculative commodity and that the highest use (the use most highly profitable for the speculator) should determine how it was to be used. The planning philosophy of the "highest use" also carried with it the built-in connotation that land use was ever changing. The only brakes communities in the L.A. region ever put on this open laissez faire-ism had to do with the sanctity of the house, of the residential use of land. Either officially by law or unofficially by agreements, certain areas,

19

generally upper-middle-class areas, were not to be invaded by the philosophy of the "highest use." Numerous enclaves—such as can be found in the communities of West L.A., Bel Air, Laughton Park, and the Los Feliz Hills; to the southwest, in Palos Verdes; or to the east and north, in San Marino and Flintridge—were effectively able to maintain their idealistic existences as residential suburbs, untainted by high density or by commercial and industrial activities.

Like the rest of the nation L.A. was hard-hit by the stock market crash and the resulting Great Depression in the early '30s. The economic effect of the Depression on L.A. can be seen in the land speculation and housing industry. In 1929, 15,234 dwelling units were constructed; in 1930 this number had fallen off to 11,257. From this point housing went into a nose dive: 6,600 units were built in 1931, and a bottom of only 1,647 units was reached in 1934.

To any objective person living during that time, these were dire figures, but L.A. has never been known for negativism and pessimism. The mayor of L.A. in the early '30s, John C. Porter, remarked that "the situation is not at all alarming;" and a writer in the Los Angeles Times was able to put the whole matter in its proper perspective when he wrote, ". . . much of the Depression is psychological."[12] Similar P.R. cover-ups were, of course, occurring across the nation; the major difference was that most people in the L.A. area never deviated from their faith in the upward-and-onward myth. This optimism was manifest in several major events that took place in the region during the early '30s. In 1931 the city celebrated its 150th anniversary with a gala 10-day Fiesta, and in July 1932 L.A. was the host to the Olympic Games, which were held in Exposition Park.[13]

L.A.'s perpetual optimism was strongly expressed in the way the city planned for its continuously growing water and energy needs. In 1928 the regional Metropolitan Water District was founded. In 1931, even with the bleakness of the Depression before them, the voters were perfectly willing to authorize the expenditure of 220 million dollars for new projects to bring water and power from the Colorado River.[14] The source of this new supply of water and electrical power was to be Hoover (Boulder) Dam on the lower Colorado River. In 1931, the Metropolitan Water District started work on the great aqueduct that was to supply the new needs of the L.A. Basin at the end of the decade. Hoover Dam was completed in 1935, and in 1936 cheap electrical power was made available to Los Angeles, so that the region lay ready and waiting for the new industrial and commercial boom that had begun in 1935. L.A.-ites were exuberant over the whole affair. Margaret Gilbert Mackey wrote in 1938: "The basin-ites will be able to enjoy their daily bath-tubfuls of water without pangs of conscience, for they will have insured all future existence on the South Coastal Plain by accomplishing what was the biggest engineering job ever undertaken in the United States."[15] The engineering statistics of the dam and the aqueduct were recited again and again, and indeed they were impressive. The aqueduct was 242 miles long, of which 92 miles were tunnels, 55 miles were conduits, and 28 miles were siphons. The main aqueduct was completed in 1938, and in 1941 it began distributing water to various participating communities. The whole system was planned to supply a projected population in the Basin of 7,500,000 people. Again, boosterism coupled with technology had succeeded.

The unswerving righteousness of the American middle-class dream was tied to the Hollywood image. The film industry proved to be one of the few durable industries. In a sense it not only weathered, but benefited from the Depression. Hollywood films provided an effective escape mechanism, and this was played to the hilt. The full-length talking films shown in neighborhood theatres were only one ingredient of the Hollywood image—the place (Sunset and Vine), the suburban environment of Beverly Hills, the life and high style of those associated with the industry were coequal components of the fantasy. The impact of the image became even stronger, in 1938, when Hollywood began large-scale radio broadcasting, for then the image could, and did, become even more a part of America's day-to-day existence.

Although the production of motion pictures remained L.A.'s chief industry throughout the '30s, the aura of Hollywood was in the long run more important for L.A.'s economic recovery during the period than was the actual number of job opportunities offered by the industry. After 1934 the film industry was joined by other economic activities that helped turn the tide, allowing L.A. to recover from the Depression in amazingly quick fashion. Oil production, long a key component in the Southern California economy, began to develop once again, especially with the expansion of production during 1936-37 in the Wilmington area. By 1936 L.A. was second to Detroit in the production of automobiles. Chrysler arrived at Maywood in 1932, Studebaker came in 1936, and General Motors opened a large plant at Southgate.

1934 can also be considered as the beginning of L.A.'s aircraft industry; by 1940, 33,000 workers were employed, and in 1941, the number increased to 120,000. By 1942, with the entrance of the U.S. into World War II, the aircraft industry in L.A. employed more workers than all other manufacturing plants combined.[16]

As would be expected, housing, land speculation, and construction in general responded strongly to the economic upturn that began in 1935. In 1932 fewer than 2,000 subdivisions were officially recorded; 1939 indicated at least a partial return to "the good old days" of the '20s with over 7,000 subdivisions recorded. In 1934 only 1,647 living units were built in the region, whereas in 1941 17,980 were constructed. No other urban locale in the U.S. came close to equaling L.A.'s economic recovery prior to 1942.

As previously mentioned, the two central ingredients of the horizontal decentralized city were the single-family detached residence and the commercial strip. During the '20s and '30s the United States perfected three forms of the strip: the urban strip, the suburban strip, and finally the highway or travelers' strip. L.A. did not invent any of these, but rather made them integral to its urban fabric in a way that was impossible for any city formed before 1920 to do.

The various strips which developed around the perimeter of other U.S. cities ended up being 20th century appendages grafted onto more traditional forms. In the traditional U.S. city, the organic growth of the urban core was predicated on increasingly higher (or more intense) land use. The automobile-oriented strips, which began to develop in the '20s, transformed this ideal into a linear, rather than a centrifugal, expression. Though the 19th century city was based on a central commercial core, inevitably one street (and not necessarily "Main Street") would emerge as the linear center of the city. The urban strip in the L.A. region developed in the same linear fashion, but on a decentralized scale never before imagined.

The preeminent urban strip of L.A. was, of course, Wilshire Boulevard, which from 1909 on, ran from downtown all the way to the sea at Santa Monica (with the one exception of Westlake Park, now MacArthur Park, which it did not cut through until 1934).[17] The commercial development of Wilshire Boulevard began in the '20s; and, by 1930, the Miracle Mile, with its posh shops, was one of the attractions of L.A. By 1941 most of the boulevard had been zoned for business activities—retail stores, movie houses, restaurants, hotels, motels, and offices. The one important exception was the two-and-one-half miles of its length in Westwood between the Los Angeles Country Club and Sepulveda Boulevard. This section developed as an exclusively upper-middle-class garden apartment strip. With this one exception, Wilshire was, as the landscape architect Ralph D. Cornell remarked, "a linear shopping district."[18]

The most prestigious commercial districts on Wilshire were the sections on both sides of Lafayette Park, the Miracle Mile and its extensions between La Brea and Fairfax Avenues, and downtown Beverly Hills. The Miracle Mile, however, housed Wilshire Boulevard's major department stores and many of its "smart" shops. Coulter's (1937) and the May Company (1940), together with surrounding shops and restaurants, made the Miracle Mile the place for the affluent to shop. The special automobile-oriented design pattern of Wilshire—the wide band of the boulevard, itself, and the placement of extensive parking areas to the rear of stores and offices—had commenced in the late '20s. As with the 1928 Bullock's Wilshire, Coulter's, the May Company, and other stores were designed to be entered from the parking area; their street entrances were quite secondary.

The city of L.A. and almost all of the surrounding communities were banded and checkerboarded by innumerable secondary urban strips. By the end of the '30s some of these strips, such as Hollywood Boulevard near Vine Street, began to assume status. Others such as Melrose Avenue and Pico Boulevard were loosely lined with single-story retail establishments and occasional nodules of supermarkets, movie houses, and two-story buildings with offices above street-level stores.

As Ralph D. Cornell noted of Hollywood, most of these strips worked "best at night when countless chromatic signs flash their iridescent pattern of color down the converging lines of their length."[19] Since many of these commercial strip streets had been laid out in the '20s and even before, their narrow width was, by the mid-'30s, considered incompatible with their new uses. Parts of Sunset, Melrose, and Pico were widened, while other major boulevards such as Olympic were not only widened but considerably extended. Although the stated purpose of these street widenings and extensions was to open up new arterial routes, everyone was well aware that such street "improvements" set the stage for eventual strip commercialization.

As the less dense commercial strips reached out into suburbia, they often became suburban, rather than urban strips. Such was the case with La Cienega at Pico, where, at the end of the '30s, a supermarket and a theatre formed a small suburban hub. The classic example of the suburban strip at the end of the '30s was Ventura Boulevard, which ran the length of the San Fernando Valley and was connected at its eastern end to Cahuenga Boulevard, the major thoroughfare over the Santa Monica Mountains. In 1930 the San Fernando Valley was sparsely settled with most of its population (54,217) at its eastern end. By 1940 its population had more than doubled (to 112,001), and developers' tracts began to emerge on both sides of Ventura Boulevard.

The boulevard, as it ran through the communities of Studio City, Sherman Oaks, Encino, Tarzana, and Woodland Hills, provided a series of localized shopping, eating, and entertainment centers. These linear suburban centers were never very large, and they were almost exclusively geared to the needs of the surrounding residential population, providing few accommodations for the highway traveler. Ventura Boulevard, consequently, never became a primary travelers' highway strip in the way that Highway 66 (mainly on Foothill Boulevard) did between San Bernardino and Pasadena.

In an article published in 1941, Richard J. Neutra observed that "crisscross communicating in all directions is more typical of Los Angeles than other of the numerous cities on four continents which the writer has visited during his studies."[20] From the early '30s on, the State Division of Highways—now the State Department of Transportation (Caltrans)—in conjunction with the Los Angeles Regional Planning Commission and the Los Angeles City Planning Commission, was actively planning and working on a system of "super" urban highways. These new highways would provide a series of transportation corridors for the private auto.

By 1941 a master plan had been adopted by the Regional Planning Commission for an extensive Metropolitan Parkway System. What was eventually to emerge as the world famous

L.A. freeway system of the late '50s and '60s was precisely outlined by Mel Scott in his 1942 volume, *Cities are for People*

> These expressways have three-hundred foot right-of ways and are beautifully landscaped along the sides with trees and shrubs. Expressways are entirely free of intersections, as all opposing routes pass over or under the roadways. Connections between routes are made by curving turning-off lanes that are depressed or elevated so that there is no interference.[21]

The first two links in the system, which were completed before the end of 1941, were the Arroyo Seco Parkway and a section of the Cahuenga Freeway (later a part of the Hollywood Freeway) over Cahuenga Pass. Extensive sections of right of way for the Santa Ana and Ramona Parkways were also acquired.[22]

Of these, the Arroyo Seco Parkway (later renamed the Pasadena Freeway) was the first. The plan for this nine-mile, double-lane parkway was first laid out in 1934; construction started in 1936 and was fully completed in 1942. As with other innovations, the West's first freeway (the term "freeway" began to crop up in 1936) followed schemes realized earlier in the East.[23] The rationale behind the Arroyo Seco Parkway set the stage for the post-World War II freeway boom in California. S.V. Cortelyou, District Engineer for the project, wrote in 1936:

> Because of the safe and quick access which the Arroyo Seco Parkway would provide to the center of Los Angeles, the areas contiguous to and served by the parkway will naturally become more desirable from a residential point of view. As a consequence, land values will be enhanced and the local business centers, which get their support almost entirely from the local residents, will receive an impetus which would come from increased population in the adjacent territories.[24]

The Arroyo Seco Parkway was quite conservative in its general design imagery. It was really thought of as part freeway and part traditional parkway. The scale and detailing of its bridges, its landscaping, and its location in the existing system of parks in the Arroyo suggested slower movement—having more to do with the conservative and traditional world of the '20s—than the freeways described in Mel Scott's 1942 volume. Of the freeway's physical features, only the concrete entrances for the tunnels through the hills of Elysian Park were styled to suggest the Streamline Moderne of the '30s.

Entirely different in feeling and scale were the two units of the Cahuenga Freeway, the first of which opened in 1940, the second in 1942.[25] Here at last was the broad, many-laned transportation corridor visualized by Scott. Eight traffic lanes, with the Pacific Electric track in the center, openly conveyed its singular purpose as a rapid transportation corridor. When Gene Autry, as the honorary Mayor of North Hollywood, helped to open the first section of the Cahuenga Freeway, Angelenos could at last experience a sample of the new world to come. The design of the bridges, retaining walls, and other features was functional and utilitarian in feeling, with just a slight hint of the Streamline Moderne. The stage was fully set for the design and pattern of the post-1945 system of freeways. (Already by 1940 one quarter of the land in the urban Los Angeles area was devoted to streets, roads, and the newly developing freeway system. Private land used for parking lots and driveways added considerably to the amount of land dedicated to the automobile.)

The suburban residential development of L.A. after 1935 occurred primarily in West L.A. (including much of the west-central Wilshire district, Hollywood, Beverly Hills, and Brentwood), the Hollywood Hills, and the San Fernando Valley. In addition several of the coastal communities—Pacific Palisades and adjacent Santa Monica Canyon, and to the south from Manhattan Beach to Newport Beach—bloomed, and by late 1941 Altadena, Sierra Madre, and Arcadia to the north and east began to experience a renewed surge of development. These L.A. suburbs of the late '30s fall roughly into types: West L.A. and the San Gabriel Valley continued their '20s image as a series of upper-middle-class retreats; the low northern slope of the Santa Monica Mountains and the flat land of the San Fernando Valley developed as middle-class suburbs; and the steep hills and canyons directly behind Hollywood, and such areas as Santa Monica Canyon and the hills in and around Silverlake, became "bohemian" suburbs.

The specifics of street patterns and land division, which formed the framework of many of these communities, had been formed in the '20s.[26] As might be expected, the upper-middle-class suburban land patterns were based on the 18th century English garden. Nature predominated, and curved and winding streets were loosely fitted into the general topography of the land. The flat land sections of West L.A. were similar to what might be found in any upper-middle-class district of an American city. There were broad streets and wide boulevards planted with rows of trees. There were expanses of lawn upon which were placed ample, usually two-story, often hidden, dwellings. Even at this early date there were swimming pools. "Amazing to Eastern visitors who chance to fly over Beverly Hills, Bel Air or Brentwood is the predominance of private swimming pools in Southern California," wrote an observer in 1940.[27] The only element that differentiated the West L.A. flat lands from those elsewhere in the U.S. were the exotic, semitropical trees and shrubs and the tendency to provide (by planting and/or walls) really usable courtyards and patios, which served as private out-of-doors living spaces.

In the lower hills and canyons, the traditional urban aspect gave way to a suggestion of the country. Winding streets became the only public connective links. Sidewalks were eliminated. Heavy plantings and fences implied that the man-made object, the dwelling, was subservient to nature. But the wildness of nature hinted at in Coldwater and Benedict Canyons was almost entirely man-made; most of it was not natural to the area.[28] Since trees and shrubs grow so rapidly in Southern California, the manipulation of outdoor spaces has often been more important than the designs of the dwellings themselves.

The middle-class suburban areas were generally situated on the flat lands or in the lower hills. In these areas in the '30s the sense of a natural, rural setting gave way to open space of vine ground cover or lawn with emphasis on single specimen, often exotic, trees and shrubs. There seemed to be a feeling that the open space was necessary to convey the impression that these houses and their grounds were just scaled-down, upper-middle-class dwellings.

In the bohemian suburbs of the Hollywood Hills and the Silverlake district, populated in part by young physicians, lawyers, and scriptwriters, untethered nature was suggested by the drama of steep hillsides and the theatrical perching of houses on precipitous slopes. Dwellings hovered over the hillsides, and heavy vegetation pressed in and around them, revealing only fragments of the man-made object, never the whole. On these steep hillsides the feel of the planting was one of untampered wilderness, almost as if a folly from an 18th century English garden had been transferred to the lotus land of Southern California.

The imagery of many of these bohemian houses was Modern, but their relationship to their environment was highly romantic and traditional.

These, then, were the facts of L.A.'s man-made physical environment of the '30s. How well was this world related to the dreams and ideals of L.A.'s professional planners and architects? Richard J. Neutra, in 1941, posed the classic question that professional planners have long directed toward L.A.: "Was this metropolis a paradise, or did there exist here a type of blight which fitted none of the classical descriptions?"[29] Professional planners tended to be of two minds. Although they wished to see L.A. traditionally, conforming to the typical strong-central-core Victorian plan of the late 19th century, they also sensed in the developing city the uniqueness of its dispersion, low density, and commitment to the automobile.

Thus, L.A. was, and still is, an enigma to members of the planning profession. The traditionalists' position was expressed in 1941 by Clifford M. Zierer, a geographer at U.C.L.A., who wrote that L.A.'s development in the late '20s and '30s "had thus far produced a sprawling, disorganized, and loosely-knit urban mass." He went on to characterize the L.A. scene with such phrases as, "disorderly sprawling" of speculative subdivisions that have "eroded" the countryside "with little or no conscious design of the city as a whole."[30] Few of the planners ever matched the keen sensitivity of the Bay area architect Michael Goodman who clearly saw that decentralized L.A. represented something which planners had never encountered before. In May 1941 he wrote:

> One can imagine the mental change in a Middle-Western woman when she dons her new pajamas to go shopping in one of the decentralized business centers of a city like Los Angeles. Here is your cue to the necessity for new styling. There is a valid sociological explanation in the fact that marginal development by the pioneers and the later arrivals has tended to produce a different culture here. When enough people are impelled by a desire of the new and the novel, they lose their umbilical attachment to their native habitat and go sailing! A new attitude is initiated. In other words, the Spirit of Eldorado is still with us.[31]

Unwilling to go "sailing," Zierer and others thumbed through the planning literature and suggested that the solution for L.A. was to be found in the turn-of-the-century Garden City Satellite communities of Ebenezer Howard.[32] So, in effect, the L.A. planners of the '30s, like many of their later counterparts, played the acrobatic game of posing as apologists for economic laissez faire-ism, while, at the same time, clothing themselves in the feudal image of the planner as a god figure, who determines what is good for the community.

Most of the inventive thinking about planning occurred, not within the planning departments of the city and the county, but from the outside. In the early '30s, Richard J. Neutra, with his younger assistants Harwell H. Harris and Gregory Ain, reformed and applied many of the ideas of Neutra's early Rush City to a regional plan for the area. The Pacific Southwest Academy, with the involvement of Mel Scott, George W. Robbins, and L. Deming Tilton, published such studies as *Los Angeles: Preface to a Master Plan* (1941) and *Cities are for People* (1942). These same individuals, organized as a Los Angeles Chapter of Telesis, worked with the Southern California Chapter of the American Institute of Architects in organizing the impressive planning exhibition held in December 1941 at Exposition Park. Of this exhibition *Time* magazine wrote:

> If the city planners could burn Los Angeles down they would rebuild it very differently. So the Los Angeles Museum decided to show the public how city planners thought the ideal city should look. With help from the County Regional Planning Commission, and a group of famous architects and designers including California's R.J. Neutra and Cranbrook Academy's Walter Baermann, the Museum's Director, balding Roland McKinney, last fortnight opened the biggest city planning show California had ever seen. They were joined by the Los Angeles Chapter of Telesis, a militant group of Pacific Coast architects who want California to look like a Lewis Mumford dreamworld. Visitors were confronted with mural blowups of ballots, marked with an X in a space labeled "better planning!" Skeptical gallery-goers realized that the ballots, too, were a dream, that Los Angeles was likely to remain its sprawling self for years.[33]

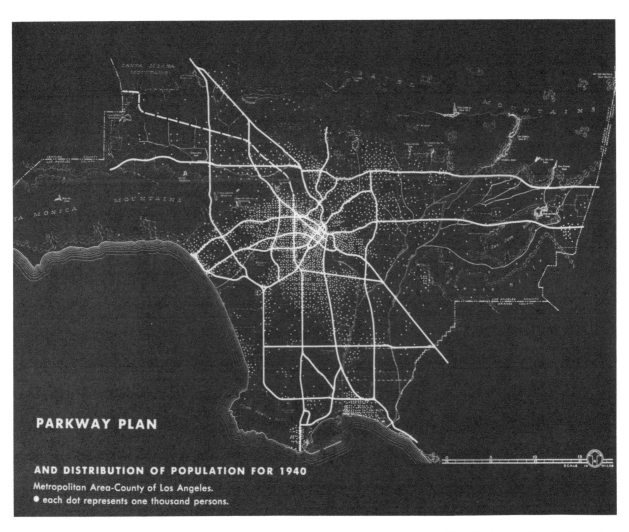

PARKWAY PLAN

AND DISTRIBUTION OF POPULATION FOR 1940
Metropolitan Area-County of Los Angeles.
● each dot represents one thousand persons.

19. Parkway Plan for Greater
     Los Angeles, 1940

25

20. Project: Conceptual design
    for urban freeways
    Los Angeles, 1941

22. Cahuenga Freeway Unit
    Los Angeles, 1940

21. Parkway System for central
    Los Angeles, 1949

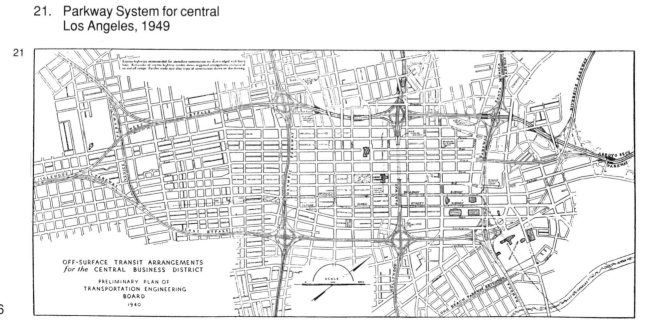

OFF-SURFACE TRANSIT ARRANGEMENTS
for the CENTRAL BUSINESS DISTRICT

PRELIMINARY PLAN OF
TRANSPORTATION ENGINEERING
BOARD
1940

SPENCE
Air Photos

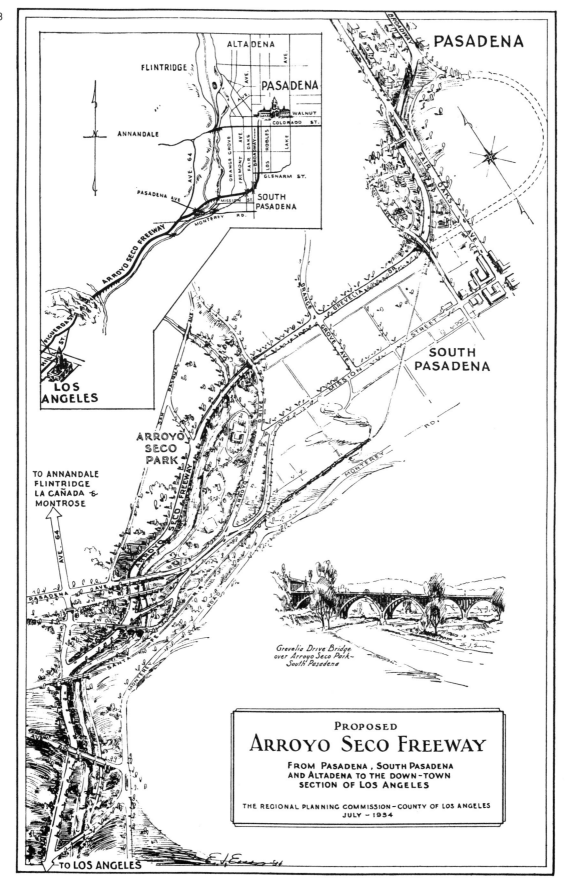

PASADENA

ALTADENA

FLINTRIDGE

PASADENA

ANNANDALE

WALNUT
COLORADO ST.

GLENARM ST.

SOUTH
PASADENA

PASADENA AVE.

MISSION ST.

MONTEREY RD.

ARROYO SECO FREEWAY

LOS
ANGELES

PASADENA

FAIR OAKS

BROADWAY

ORANGE GROVE DR.

GREVELIA DR.

STREET

SOUTH
PASADENA

MONTEREY

RD.

ARROYO
SECO
PARK

TO ANNANDALE
FLINTRIDGE
LA CAÑADA &
MONTROSE

AVE. 64

PASADENA AVE

ARROYO SECO FREEWAY

ARROYO

MISSION

ORANGE GROVE AVE.

SAN PASQUAL

DRIVE

SANTA FE

MONTEREY

AVE 99

Grevelia Drive Bridge
over Arroyo Seco Park~
South Pasadena

TO LOS ANGELES

PROPOSED
ARROYO SECO FREEWAY
FROM PASADENA, SOUTH PASADENA
AND ALTADENA TO THE DOWN-TOWN
SECTION OF LOS ANGELES

THE REGIONAL PLANNING COMMISSION—COUNTY OF LOS ANGELES
JULY - 1934

23. Arroyo Seco Parkway
    Proposed plan
    Los Angeles, 1934

24. Arroyo Seco Parkway
    Under construction, 1939

25. Arroyo Seco Parkway
    In use, 1941

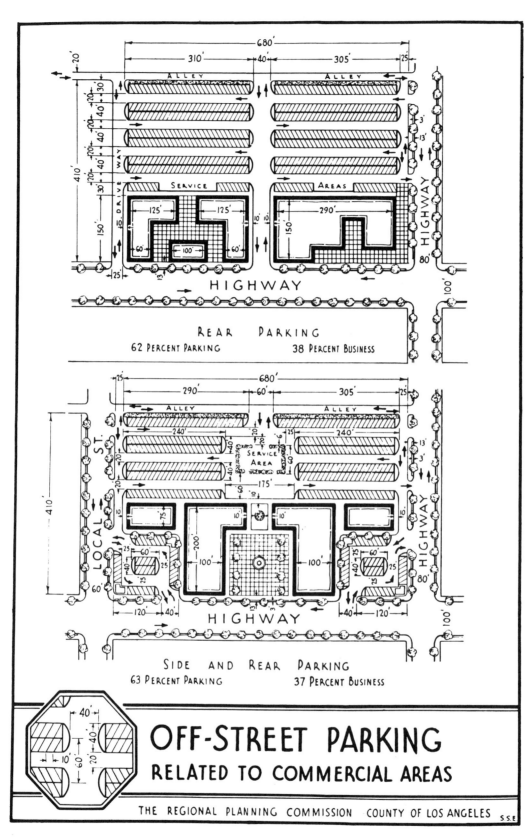

OFF-STREET PARKING
RELATED TO COMMERCIAL AREAS

THE REGIONAL PLANNING COMMISSION   COUNTY OF LOS ANGELES

26.   Project: Concept for off-street parking
      for retail commercial buildings
      Los Angeles, 1941

30

COMMERCIAL

THE IMAGERY EMPLOYED for L.A.'s commercial architecture of the '30s mirrored the shifts in architectural fashion occurring throughout the U.S. during this decade. The region's commercial building also reflected the changing patterns of use, especially those changes brought about by the automobile. That "super-charged mechanism" pressed architects and clients to adopt new forms of drive-in architecture. It forced designers to come up with new packaging, based not on the traditional slow impact of a building on the pedestrian, but rather on how to impinge on a viewer as he speeded past and, hopefully, to persuade him to enter the establishment in his private capsule. Referring to L.A.'s new commercial architecture, Henry-Russell Hitchcock noted in 1940:

> Nothing in the East compares with the best of this sort in Los Angeles, if only because Eastern cities have not the motorized planning which has been achieved apparently without conscious direction.[34]

As to the specifics of imagery, L.A. architects partially discarded the favored packaging of the '20s, the Spanish Colonial Revival and the Zig-zag Moderne or Art Deco, replacing these earlier garments with the Streamline Moderne, the "Hollywood Regency," and a loose and inventive interpretation of the eastern Anglo-Colonial Revival. The curved surfaces, horizontal emphases, portholes, and glass brick of the Streamline Moderne made it plain that here indeed was the future. The Hollywood Regency played a delightful stylistic tightrope game. It was traditional, suggesting delicacy and refinement, but it was also so simplified in details, surfaces, and volume as to be modern at the same time—the best, in

other words, of the two worlds. The general approach which Los Angeles architects took to the Anglo-Colonial was to look toward what was then referred to as the "Colonial Farm House," particularly the Colonial buildings found in and around Philadelphia. In addition these architects also "Colonialized" (i.e., added Colonial details to) such regional images as that of the Monterey and the developing single-story California Ranch House.

There were, of course, other odds and ends of styling to be found in the commercial architecture of L.A. in the '30s. While the urge to recreate Spain and the Mediterranean in California was no longer pursued with as great a passion as it had been in the '20s, there were a number of smaller buildings constructed in the '30s that still reflected the Hispanic myth. The style favored as the continuator of the myth was the Monterey, often stripped down like the Regency to give a hint that modernity was, indeed, important. Finally, there were, in and around L.A., a group of commercial buildings that were Modern rather than Moderne—offices and retail store buildings by R.M. Schindler, Richard J. Neutra, Gregory Ain, and others.

As a general rule, most of the smaller commercial buildings, regardless of style, were either of exposed concrete or were clothed in cement stucco. This meant that differences between them were not always great, and also that the buildings of the '30s mixed relatively easily with those of the '20s, giving L.A.'s commercial architecture a remarkably unified appearance. In older, more traditional U.S. cities, the new Modern or Moderne buildings, especially if sheathed in white stucco or painted concrete, clashed openly with the older structures around them.

America's new arbiters of taste in the '30s, the industrial designers, convinced manufacturers, retailers, and above all, the middle- and upper-middle-class public, that it was essential to repackage products varying from food to automobiles. Especially in the early years of the Depression (from 1933 through 1936), the "modernization" of buildings was avidly pursued, not necessarily, it should be noted, to improve their functioning, but to transform their images into something which was "smart and up-to-date." Los Angeles experienced more than its share of this revamping of imagery. One of the most notable examples was the 1906 Philharmonic Auditorium Building, which was transformed from modified Gothic to Moderne architecture by Claud Beelman (1938).

Between 1931 and 1941, as the growing commitment to the automobile and the commercial strip pushed clients and architects into the new realm of drive-in architecture, L.A. began to blossom with a full array of drive-in buildings, ranging from department stores and supermarkets to drive-in theatres, hot dog stands, restaurants, banks, laundries, shoe repair shops, and florists. Mel Scott referred to all of this as "motorized living," and indeed it was.[35] While none of these new forms of drive-in architecture was necessarily invented in L.A., it was L.A., in the '30s, that perfected these forms, which were to become the dominant building types for the post-World War II linear city.

Most popular and widespread of the drive-ins were the supermarkets or, as they were referred to in the late '30s, "supers." By late 1938, "half a dozen or more new supermarkets were entering the Southern California scene each month."[36] As a designed object, these late '30s L.A. supermarkets had pretty well arrived at a set solution. In style they were Streamline Moderne; the body of the building was a horizontal box opened, both to the street and to the parking lot, by a continuous band of horizontal plate-glass windows. At one corner, dominating the whole, was a huge "festoonal tower"—not a tower in the traditional sense, but actually a vertical sign.[37] Externally, this sign was *it;* the building was a stucco box, which, like other Moderne objects of the '30s, had been "styled" by the surface appliqué of thin planes and lines. The canopy-covered entrance faced onto the parking lot, not the street.

Stiles O. Clements, especially in his numerous stores for the Ralphs Grocery Company, created the most impressive group of these structures.[38] The Ralphs supermarket in Inglewood was a perfect example of the transformation of a building into a sign. The face of the sign was perpendicular to the street and parallel to the parking lot entrance of the building; there is no doubt about which façade was the major one.

The necessity to serve the automobile led to the continual transformation of older building types into drive-in forms. The first of the drive-in banks was built in 1937, in Vernon, by the Security-First National Bank (designed by Reed McClure). "In its newly-opened Vernon branch, which is the only 'Drive-in Bank' in the world, the Security-First National Bank of Los Angeles may have uncovered for the building industry a vast new field of bank construction."[39]

The motion-picture theatre was another building type that changed in response to the automobile. In 1933, Richard M. Hollingshead, Jr. obtained a patent for the drive-in motion-picture theatre and opened America's first in Camden, New Jersey. America's second drive-in theatre (licensed by Hollingshead's company, Park-In Theaters), opened in 1934 at the corner of Pico and Westwood Boulevards.[40]

Though L.A. was early on the scene with the drive-in theatre, this form did not fully come into its own until after 1945. The enclosed auditorium situated in the suburbs remained the preferred form of theatre during the '30s. It was S. Charles Lee, in his 1931 Florence Theatre, who first oriented the theatre both to the strip and to the automobile, as the major method of reaching and entering the theatre. In the Florence Theatre, Lee provided a motor driveway which gave entrance first to the enclosed forecourt and then to the parking lot in the rear.[41] He repeated this theme in a number of theatres during the '30s, the most successful of which was the 1939 Academy Theatre in Inglewood. As with the supermarket, the new auto-oriented theatre of the '30s was a sculptural sign with its minimal box behind. Even more than the supermarket, the theatre was styled by neon and incandescent lights. At night only three facets of the Academy Theatre were visible: the tower with its lettering and spiral form, the marquee with advertising above and entrance below, and finally the spiral parking sign to the side.

A similar and equally effective approach was taken by other architects. Paul Laszlo, in his 1939 Crenshaw Theatre, extended the marquee to the side so that theatregoers could be let off and picked up under cover (with the auto parked in the adjoining parking lot); and Gordon B. Kaufmann, one of L.A.'s impressive exponents of period architecture, designed the 1937 Earl Carroll Theatre in Hollywood to face entirely onto its side parking area. At night the building disappeared, leaving only the outline of a woman's head, the repeated lettering of the theatre's name, and the lighted horizontal band of the marquee and its extended porte-cochere, which united building and parking lot.

Though the Streamline Moderne image became the norm for theatres throughout the Los Angeles area, their interiors continued to make reference to ornaments, forms, and curved surfaces associated with the late '20s Art Deco. By the end of the '30s, however, S. Charles Lee and others were beginning to shift theatre interiors from the appearance of futuristic machines to the flamboyant world of motion-picture Baroque.

The imagery that has been used for L.A.'s restaurants is one of Southern California's major contributions to 20th century architecture, both high and low. It was during the '20s that L.A. experienced her first golden age of programmatic buildings, ranging from igloos, which served ice cream, and Egyptian sphinxes, which sold real estate, to enlarged flower pots, which marketed cut flowers and plants. These little buildings conveyed their message by transforming the whole building into a symbolic sign for their products, an overall transformation aimed not at the pedestrian, but at the customer in his automobile.

The renaissance of programmatic architecture was regrettably brief, and it was for the most part a product of the late '20s, not the '30s.[42] There is at least one notable exception. Marcus P. Miller, who helped bring the Streamline Moderne to numerous retail stores, especially along the Miracle Mile, created one of Los Angeles' most memorable programmatic buildings, the Darkroom (1938) on Wilshire Boulevard, a photographic shop in the form of a streamline camera. Most of the programmatic creatures of the '20s somehow managed to survive into the '30s, however, as ruins or objects still in use; and some, like the Brown Derby of 1926, remained as major local and tourist attractions.

At the end of the '20s, L.A.'s inventiveness expanded in other directions, one of which was the development of the quick-snack drive-in. These structures tended to be more staid than the earlier programmatic structures. The favored fashions in 1930 were the Spanish Colonial Revival or the Zigzag Moderne; by 1935 the Streamline Moderne became the *in* style. The stylistic evolution of the Carpenters Drive-Ins provides a good illustration of the changes that came about from the '20s on through the '30s. The L-shaped 1929 Carpenters Drive-In is respectably Spanish; the 1935 Carpenters is transitional Moderne—somewhere between the Zigzag and the Streamline; while the circular 1937 Carpenters on Sunset Boulevard comes out in full force for the Streamline Moderne. L.A.'s drive-ins of the late '20s acknowledged the automobile, but basically retained the more traditional image of a restaurant as an indoor eating place. Those of the '30s, like Carpenters Sunset Drive-In or the projected 1935 Roadside Restaurant (designed by Kem Weber), were planned so that the patron could eat in his car. The "architecture" of these late '30s drive-ins was reduced to three elements: a dominant sign, which could easily be read day or night from the street; a small enclosed counter-kitchen area, which might or might not have eating space inside; and a cantilevered canopy, which not only provided shelter from the weather, but also visually tied the small enclosed area to the moveable automobile capsules. By late 1941, drive-ins had popped up on all of L.A.'s strips.

Equally catholic in their locations were motels and service stations. The horizontal, low-density land use, even on such urban strips as Wilshire Boulevard, meant that drive-ins, motels, and service stations could be, and were, built anywhere and everywhere. Most of the L.A. motels were not built as accommodations primarily for tourists traveling from one location to another. By far the majority of pre-1942 motels were designed as small, automobile-oriented, urban hotels. Hollywood was filled with them. Others, such as the Motor Inn (George R. and Samuel Postel, 1938), were built in such distant communities as Arcadia, to accommodate visitors to the new Santa Anita Park Racetrack, which opened Christmas Day 1934; or, like Carl's Sea Air Cafe and Motel in Santa Monica (Burton A. Schutt, 1938), to accommodate users of the nearby beach.[43]

R.M. Schindler's projected Highway Bungalow Hotel of 1931 showed what the "ideal" motel should include: sleeping rooms, a restaurant of the drive-in variety, and, if possible, a service station. And while the clientele of each of these three overlapped, it was considered ideal that each be independent and attract its own patrons. 33

For instance, the open-air and enclosed restaurant at Carl's Sea Air Cafe was undoubtedly of more economic importance than the 10-plus rooms of the motel.

Though one hundred percent committed to the auto, L.A.'s service station imagery remained surprisingly conservative throughout the '30s. As elsewhere in the U.S., the preferred image was that of a pristine industrial product—by the late '30s a steel frame sheathed in porcelainized metal panels. Signs tended to be reticent, compared to other drive-in buildings. They consisted of lettering on the building and on the projecting canopy, perhaps a roof sign, and then a separate, free-standing pole sign (sometimes supplemented by a billboard). As an example of a factory-produced industrial product, the L.A. service station of the late '30s was the building type that came closest to expressing the mechanistic imagery held so dear by the proponents of Modern architecture. L.A. made no particular contribution to the design of the service station as such; its only unique contribution had to do with the sheer number of them built during the '30s and their dispersal throughout the whole of the L.A. Basin.

Considering the larger department store buildings, Henry-Russell Hitchcock noted during his 1940 visit to L.A.: "Even a large Department Store like that of the May Co. on Wilshire, by its isolation and by the skill of its adaptation to an open site has virtues which similar stylistically 'modern' commercial architecture has hardly achieved elsewhere . . . ."[44] Albert C. Martin's 1940 May Company store, to which Hitchcock was referring, applied the lessons learned in supermarket design to a large-scale building.[45] The corner gold tower (a real '30s perfume bottle) with its lettered sign dominated the architecture of the building, especially when lighted at night. The horizontal bands of projecting, metal-framed windows and the thin sheathing of travertine served as a neutral backdrop for the corner tower. Though opening to the street, the store's major entrance lay toward its extensive parking lot, situated on the side of the building away from Wilshire Boulevard.

A few blocks east on Wilshire was Stiles O. Clements' Coulter's Department Store of 1937, which was, like the May Company, oriented to its rear parking lot.[46] Coulter's represented a different design viewpoint from the May Company. Here the insistent Moderne styling of the entire building was meant to convey more openly the image of the store's hoped-for upper-middle-class clientele. Equally highly styled was the 1940 Broadway-Pasadena by Albert B. Gardner, which, like Coulter's and the May Company, boasted a major canopy-covered entrance facing its 400-car parking lot.[47] The imagery of the May Company was addressed to a wide middle-class audience, while Coulter's and the Broadway-Pasadena, as befitted their upper-middle-class clientele, were more low-key and selfconsciously sophisticated.

The store that most openly embraced the auto was the 1938 Sears Roebuck store on Pico Boulevard designed by John S. Redden and John G. Raben. When it was described in the *Architectural Forum* in 1940, the editors wrote: "An important part of Sears Roebuck merchandising policy is the provision for parking space, and in this new store for Los Angeles this has been expressed in a dramatic fashion."[48] Taking advantage of the slope of the site, the design provided three levels of parking, one of which was on the roof of the main building. Various functions of the building were broken up and scattered around the site. There was a separate outdoor sales building, a service station, an auto center, and "points were provided in each parking area where heavy articles can be picked up and transferred to the cars."[49] Though the architects claimed that their sole concern was merchandising, the building ended up being a sensitive version of the Streamline Moderne style.

Another building type that had to make elaborate provisions for the auto was the racetrack. Two very fashionable ones were built in the L.A. area in the '30s: Santa Anita Park in Arcadia (Gordon B. Kaufmann, 1934) and the Hollywood Turf Club in Inglewood (Stiles O. Clements, 1937).[50] Both set aside acres of land for parking, and both sought to impress their users with their high styling: Kaufmann's was "modern Georgian," while Clements' was modish Streamline Moderne. Kaufmann's wonderful inventiveness in dealing with traditional forms is evident in the horizontal screens of cut-out metal that line the loggias situated at the rear of the grandstand. Some of these screens show scenes of racing horses, others show groups of palm trees.[51]

Places of entertainment had, of necessity, to provide for automobile parking. The city's most widely known Streamline Moderne building, the 1935 Pan-Pacific Auditorium (Charles F. Plummer, Walter Wurdeman, and Welton Becket), along with its associated open-air

"Theatre of the Stars," devoted much of it site to automobile parking. When, a few years later (1938), a second enclosed arena was proposed (designed by Samuel E. Lunden), additional land was to be acquired for parking. When Myron Hunt and H.C. Chambers designed the new Palomar Sports Center (1940) at Third Street and Vermont Avenue, they devoted 12 acres of the 18-acre site to parking. In Hollywood, Gordon B. Kaufmann's Paladium Ballroom (1940) on Sunset Boulevard oriented its principal entrance to the adjoining parking lot. While both the Palomar and the Paladium were committed to the Streamline Moderne image, their interiors were characterized by a sense of stage-set Baroque and Rococo.

In 1939, Los Angeles acquired an additional public extravaganza (considering the place and its mild climate). This was Westwood Village's outdoor Tropical Ice Garden. The stage set for this extravaganza contrasted the suggestions of cut-out northwoods pine trees with tropical tile roofed Spanish buildings.[52]

The more traditional side of L.A.'s commercial architecture is best seen in Gordon Kaufmann's Los Angeles Times Building of 1931-35 and in Albert R. Walker and Percy A. Eison's Sunkist (California Fruit Growers Exchange) Building of 1935. The evolution of the design for the Los Angeles Times Building dramatically mirrors the change in taste from the late '20s to the early '30s. Kaufmann's first design was for a Spanish-clothed structure; this design was replaced by one which played off the perpendicularism of the Art Deco with many interior details that looked to the Streamline Moderne.

The Sunkist Building is in what could be called the "American Perpendicular style." With its monumental flavor, the Classical bent in its piers and capitals, its relief sculpture and entrance murals, it could seemingly be, with a mere change of name, a perfect P.W.A. (Public Works Administration) Moderne government building of the '30s. However, there were differences. The Sunkist Building was designed to be entered from an automobile, and its interior air conditioning and posh offices created an internal world not to be found in a P.W.A. product.

Out on Sunset Boulevard, away from downtown, were two buildings that attracted the out-of-town tourist: the N.B.C. Building of 1938-39 by John C. Austin Co., and the C.B.S. Building of 1937-38 by New York architect William Lescaze and E.T. Heitschmidt. Both employed the symbolic styling of the Moderne; however, the N.B.C. Building, low in scale, but suggesting the monumental by its corner pavilion, was more indicative of the L.A. architectural temperament. The C.B.S. Building, like almost all of Lescaze's work, was a mixture of the Streamline Moderne and the Modern—in this case the International Style. Of the two buildings, it is by far the more serious in its high-art pretension. But to the average visitor, the N.B.C. Building projected a more sensitive reaction to its environs. Behind a long row of tall palm trees on Sunset Boulevard was a low terrace partially sheltered by a canopy, and beyond this were three major N.B.C. studio spaces. This low, block-long building was able to emerge from the ordinary and be distinctive and impressive, yet at the same time it did not conflict with the drive-ins and other buildings surrounding it.

The neutral white stucco box had been an essential ingredient of L.A. architecture since the days of the Mission Revival in the early 1900s. By the late '30s it had discarded its earlier historic garments and fully embraced the Moderne. The stucco box could be transformed into the new by the slightest touch: a band of horizontal windows, a curved wall leading into an entrance, and, by use of that hallmark of the '30s Moderne, the glass brick. Most concrete stucco boxes—for factories, warehouses, and similar uses—were small, seldom over two stories high. A few were larger, like the five-story Bekins Storage Building in L.A. (1940), or the extensive Kem Weber–designed Walt Disney Studios complex in Burbank (1939-40).[53]

Sometimes white stucco or concrete was molded, not into a neutral box, but into something highly programmatic. In 1937 Robert V. Derrah designed the Coca-Cola Bottling Plant on Central Avenue as a concrete ship wherein symbols became rich and complex. The ocean liner equaled the machine and was, therefore, appropriate for the conveyor belt production of bottles of Coke. The hygienic nature of the modern steel ship was equated to the hygienic needs of a modern bottling company. And the aerodynamic streamlining of the ocean liner was captured in the stationary concrete building. The obliqueness of this sort of symbolism is apparent only to the academic mind; for the public it was good public relations, and it all made sense.[54]

Derrah again used the ship (this time crowned by a tower and a lighted, turning ball, representing the world) as a centerpiece for his 1936 shopping center, Crossroads of the World, on Sunset Boulevard.[55] Again the symbolism of the ship was readable by all. Its form dramatically contrasted with the "Continental" Village to the rear. There the image of Mexico and Spain was played off against Italian, French, Moorish, and Turkish forms, and the whole complex reached its conclusion in a lighthouse.

The past was used programmatically in the well-known Farmer's Market, which opened in 1934. The imagery here was half Midwestern farm and half a gentle hint at a frontier village. Derrah's eye-attracting tower with its revolving ball was World's Fair-ish and machinelike; the Farmer's Market's windmill, with the name of the establishment on the weathervane, was suburban and rural.

Larger single-level industrial buildings, constructed in and around L.A. from the mid-'30s on, were generally clean and simple in design, tending as a rule toward the Streamline, but not heavily styled. Four major industrial/distribution buildings and complexes were built in the late 1930s in the community of Vernon. One was H.H. Brunnier's Owens-Illinois Pacific Building (1937), which, befitting its product, was a virtual curved-corner glass-brick box. Nearby, the Aluminum Company of America building, designed by Gordon B. Kaufmann (1938), is a finely detailed design, which plays off the Streamline Moderne against the more monumental classical P.W.A. Moderne. Certainly the most dramatically insistent Streamline Moderne industrial building in the L.A. area was that of the Lane-Wells Company (1938-39). In William E. Myers' design of this building one sees the early '30s sketches of the New York industrial designer Norman Bel Geddes brought to fulfillment. Finally, the California Walnut Growers Association Warehouse (1935) was basically an enclosed space from the ground; from the air its central raised roof (to accommodate freight cars) and its clear pattern of skylights brought it close to the then-current work which Albert Kahn's firm was doing in and around Detroit.[56]

The great surge of large-scale industrial construction started in 1940 and is best seen in the aircraft plants built in the flat lands south of L.A. and in the San Fernando Valley. These plants covered immense acreages, and their designs were all purposely utilitarian and neutral. When, on occasion, a plant's office wing was styled, it was always streamlined. This was the case with Gordon B. Kaufmann's Vultee Aircraft plant in Downey, John and Donald B. Parkinson's Vega Aviation plant in Burbank, and E.S. Kittrich

Co.'s Northrop Aircraft plant in Hawthorne (all 1940).[57] Since the plant sites were huge (Northrop had a 73-acre site), the architects devoted as much design time to the acres of parking and to the access roads as they did to the buildings themselves.

Although Streamline Moderne was the dominant style after 1935, historically derived designs continued to be used because of their strong symbolic implications. Elegant shops and stores— Beverly Hills' I. Magnin Co. (Myron Hunt and H.C. Chambers, 1939), Saks Fifth Avenue (John and Donald B. Parkinson, with interiors by Paul R. Williams, 1937), and the Max Factor Building (S. Charles Lee, 1935) conveyed their exclusiveness by their staged and refined design, a mixture of Classical, Regency, and just a slight touch of Moderne.[58] Kaufmann emphasized the same chaste Regency-Classical in his Library of the L.A. County Medical Association (1934), while Paul R. Williams created an elegant 18th century Georgian country house (together with an impressive walled formal garden) for the Music Corporation of America Building in Beverly Hills in 1939.[59]

The styling of the most elegant of these commercial buildings, in the hands of George Vernon Russell and Gordon B. Kaufmann, gradually began to change by the late '30s. One approach fused the Regency with the Streamline Moderne, producing such light and delicate buildings as the Star's Dressing Room at the Twentieth Century–Fox Studios (Russell, 1936) or the William Morris Agency (Russell, 1939) in Beverly Hills. But at the same time these two designers were anticipating post-1945 styling by eschewing the imagery of both the Streamline and the Regency in favor of the neutral box, or series of boxes. This approach was evidenced in Russell's 1936 remodeling of Ciro's Restaurant on Sunset Boulevard and in Kaufmann's 1938 Myron Selznick and Company building (with interiors by Paul T. Frankl).

Rows of low, single-floor shops, vaguely Anglo-Colonial, with projecting Regency bay windows, lined a number of blocks of Sunset Boulevard and other principal boulevards.[60] The Colonial image was also the preferred fashion for upper-middle-class decorators' shops, as is evident in Charles O. Matcham's design for the Studios of Chessewrite, Mason and Co.(1939). The Colonial implied, as did the Regency, that the establishments it housed were more than just run-of-the-mill. The Colonial Drive-In (c. 1933), with its two-story Mt. Vernon porch, was not just any drive-in, nor was the early imagery of the Trocadero Cafe on Sunset Boulevard that of just any restaurant.

The exotic play-world of Hawaii and the South Pacific began to appear with increased frequency, especially for restaurants and theatres. The most famous of these was Don the Beachcomber's Restaurant (c. 1937), which used its open porches, bamboo fences, and heavy "tropical" vegetation to suggest programmatically the exotic world of a tropical island. Such use of imagery to convey atmosphere was taken up with a vengeance after 1945.

The architecture of small shops, bowling alleys, and restaurants changed almost as rapidly during the '30s as did the automobile, which was restyled yearly. In 1936 George Vernon Russell remodeled the Colonial Trocadero Restaurant to a new Regency-Moderne image so it could better suggest the Hollywood illusion of sophisticated, black-tie nightlife. And on fashionable Rodeo Drive in Beverly Hills, Russell and Douglas Honnold designed a row of six shops (including the Frankl Galleries) with individual façades like picture frames hung on the interior walls of a fashionable Beverly Hills residence.

The true died-in-the-wool Modernists—such architects as R.M. Schindler, Richard J. Neutra, and Gregory Ain—played only a marginal role in L.A.'s commercial architecture of the '30s. The imagery of these Modernists, furthermore, did not represent anything approaching a unified point of view. And although they—together with their counterparts from Frank Lloyd Wright on—delighted in trying their hands at designing service stations, no Modernist was actually able to realize a built service station until after World War II. A competition sponsored by the Union Oil Company prompted Schindler to submit a design "constructed of steel, glass and plants," which certainly would have attracted the attention of the passing motorist. Two years later Schindler designed another service station featuring an open two-story, post-and-beam, false-front façade that, in good L.A. fashion, became both the architecture and the sign.

Among the Modernists, Schindler and Ain both designed small medical buildings. Ain's Brownfield Medical Building of 1938-39 came very close to transforming the Modern into the commercial vernacular; Schindler's Sunset Medical Building of 1936 was a styled, high-art object, presenting a low, sculptured façade of interlocking planes comprised of stucco walls, different patterns of glass brick, and signs.

Neutra's 1930s Universal Pictures (Laemmle) Building and his Scholts Advertising Building of 1937 symbolized the building as a designed machine. The very different courses pursued by Neutra and Schindler continued on throughout the '30s. Neutra's project for a Multi-Story Parking Garage in 1940 sought to equate the Modern with technology. Schindler continued to consider art first and technology second as is apparent in his 1932 Sardi's Restaurant and in his 1937-38 Modern Creator's Shops, both in Hollywood, and his 1939-40 group of shops and offices on Ventura Boulevard for the developer William Lingenbrink. The latter two projects indicate how Schindler could play with projecting and receding stuccoed surfaces to create startling compositions which served as their own eye-catching advertisements.

Equally marginal to the mainstream International Style Modern of the '30s was the work of Lloyd Wright. Like Schindler, his approach to function and image recognized the complexity inherent in each project. The visual impact of his 1931 project for a Drive-In Open Air Market and Restaurant was designed for the auto; the low horizontal roof of the drive-in and the gigantic eye-catching sign could not help but attract attention. This open recognition of the L.A. atmosphere on Wright's part was equally evident in his Westlake Medical Building of 1935 and in his projected Motor Court of 1937.

J.R. Davidson received more commissions for retail stores and offices than any other Modernist during the decade.[61] His general approach was more strongly rational, sophisticated, and elegant than that of the other Modernists. In 1937 he redesigned Schindler's Sardi's Restaurant, bringing its imagery more up to date; and in 1941, his Feingold and Harris Medical Building on Wilshire indicated the direction in which Modern commercial design would go in the late '40s and the '50s.

Raphael Soriano followed a path in his few projects for commercial buildings somewhat similar to that of Davidson, except that he, like Schindler, had a nontraditional—i.e., non-Beaux Arts—sense of scale and proportion, which was often quite jarring. Harwell H. Harris, in his one realized commercial building of the '30s, the Grandview Gardens Restaurant of 1940, rejected the Modern imagery and suggested the Orient through an enlarged, gable-roofed California bungalow. Like Davidson, he was indicating another path that the imagery of post-World War II commercial architecture would follow.

27

27. Carpenters Drive-In
    Hollywood, 1935
28. Carpenters Drive-In
    c. 1929

38

29. Harrold's Drive-In
    Beverly Hills, c. 1936
30. Colonial Drive-In
    Hollywood, c. 1939

31

32

40

31. Motor Inn
    George R. and Samuel Postel
    Arcadia, 1938

32. Ambassodor Hotel, Swimming Pool
    Los Angeles, 1938

33. Slapsy Maxie's Restaurant
    Hollywood, c. 1937

34. Trocadero Cafe
    Hollywood, 1933

THRU THESE PORTALS PASS THE MOST BEAUTIFUL GIRLS IN THE WORLD

EARL CARROLL

$2.50 - INCLUDES LAVISH REVUE - DINNER - DANCING

THEAT
"RESTAUR

35. Earl Carroll Theatre
    Gordon B. Kaufmann
    Hollywood, 1937

36

37

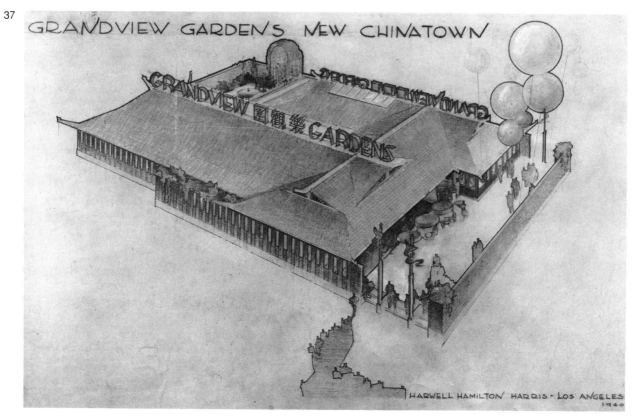

44

36. Don the Beachcomber Restaurant
    Hollywood, c. 1937

37. Grandview Gardens Restaurant
    Harwell H. Harris
    Los Angeles, 1940

38. Sardi's Restaurant
    R.M. Schindler
    Hollywood, 1932

39. Laemmle Office Building
    Richard J. Neutra
    Los Angeles, 1933

40. Cashis King Supermarket
    Hollywood, c.1931

41. Sunfax Mart
    Hollywood, 1933

42. Los Feliz Mart
    H. Roy Kelley
    Hollywood, 1933

43. Ralphs Supermarket
    Stiles O. Clements
    Inglewood, 1940

44

45

48

44. Mobil Service Station
Los Angeles, c. 1934

45. Project: Union Oil Station
R.M. Schindler
Los Angeles, 1932

46. "Miracle Mile" on
Wilshire Boulevard
Los Angeles, 1941

47. Hollywood Boulevard
Hollywood, 1942

48

49

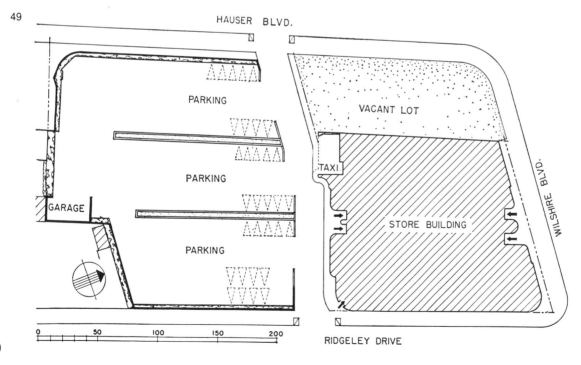

HAUSER BLVD.

PARKING

PARKING

GARAGE

PARKING

0   50   100   150   200

RIDGELEY DRIVE

VACANT LOT

TAXI

STORE BUILDING

WILSHIRE BLVD.

50

48. Coulter's Department Store
    Stiles O. Clements
    Los Angeles, 1937

49. Coulter's Department Store
    Site plan

50. Coulter's Department Store
    Parking lot entrance

51. Stores on Ventura Blvd. for
    William Lingenbrink
    R.M. Schindler
    North Hollywood, 1939-40

52. May Company department store
    on Wilshire Boulevard
    (Photograph includes site plan)
    Albert Martin and S.A. Marx
    Los Angeles, 1940

53. Project: Retail store building
    Paul R. Williams
    Beverly Hills, c. 1939

54. I. Magnin and Company store
    Myron Hunt and H.C. Chambers
    Beverly Hills, 1939

55. The Darkroom
    Marcus P. Miller
    Los Angeles, 1938

56. Farmer's Market
    Los Angeles, 1937

57.-59. Crossroads of the World
    Robert V. Derrah
    Hollywood, 1936

60. Project: Retail stores and office building
    Stiles O. Clements
    Los Angeles, 1937

61. Max Factor Building
    S. Charles Lee
    Hollywood, 1931

62. Farmers Automobile Inter-Insurance
    Exchange Building
    Albert R. Walker and Percy A. Eisen
    Los Angeles, 1937

63. Republic Insurance Company Building
Robert Field, Jr. (Field and Hoak)
Los Angeles, 1940-41

64. Sunkist (California Fruit Growers Exchange)
Building
Albert R. Walker and Percy A. Eison
Los Angeles, 1935

65. Los Angeles Times Building
Gordon B. Kaufmann
Los Angeles, 1931-35

66. Sunset Medical Building
    R.M. Schindler
    Hollywood, 1936

67.-69. Coca-Cola Bottling Company
    Robert V. Derrah
    Los Angeles, 1937

70. Bekins Storage Building
Los Angeles, 1940

71. V.E.G.A. Aviation plant
John and Donald B. Parkinson
Burbank, 1949

72. Vultee Aircraft Inc. plant
Gordon B. Kaufmann
Downey, 1940

73. California Walnut Growers
Association warehouse
Albert C. Martin
Los Angeles, 1935

71

70

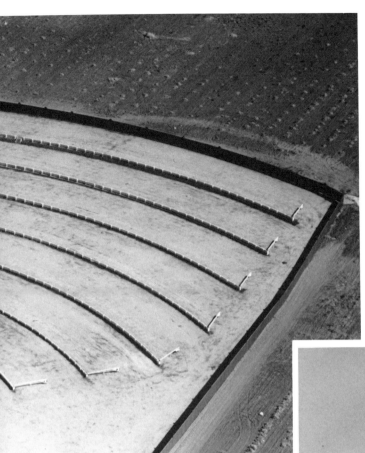

74. Drive-In Theatre
Corner of Pico and
Westwood Boulevards
Los Angeles, 1934

75. Academy Theatre
S. Charles Lee
Inglewood, 1939

76. Walt Disney Studios
    Kem Weber
    Burbank, 1939-40

77. Walt Disney Studios
    Street sign
    Kem Weber

78. Walt Disney Studios
    Director's office
    Kem Weber

79. R.K.O. Radio Pictures Studios
    Hollywood, 1935

80. Twentieth Century–Fox Studios
    Star's Dressing Room
    George Vernon Russell
    Hollywood, 1936

81. Music Corporation of America
    Paul R. Williams
    Beverly Hills, 1940

82. Columbia Studios
    Motion-picture lot
    Hollywood, 1938

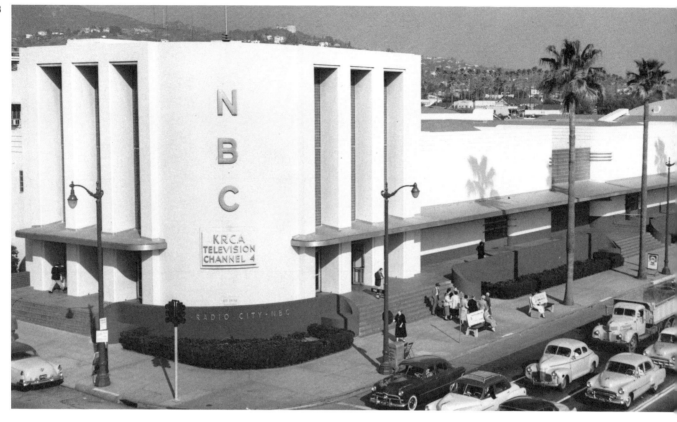

83. National Broadcasting Company Building
John C. Austin Co.
Hollywood, 1938-39

84.-85. Columbia Broadcast System Building
William Lescaze and E.T. Heitschmidt
Hollywood, 1937-38

86. Outdoor Ice Skating Rink
    Wayne D. McAlister
    Lakewood Village, 1939

87. Pan-Pacific Auditorium
    Charles F. Plummer, Walter Wurdeman,
    and Welton Becket
    Hollywood, 1935

88. Santa Anita Park
    Rear of grandstand
    Gordon B. Kaufmann
    Santa Anita, 1935

89.-90. Project: Art
Center School
Kem Weber
Los Angeles,
1934-36

89

90

74

PUBLIC

ANGELENOS OF THE '30s enjoyed a literal renaissance of public architecture. Federal funds, mostly parceled out through the Public Works Administration or the Post Office Department, encouraged county and city governments and school districts to engage in large-scale building programs. Between 1933 and 1939 the P.W.A. provided the state of California with funds for over 221 government buildings and 140 schools, and a lion's share of these buildings were constructed in Southern California.[62] In addition, other projects, such as new post offices and public housing, were federally funded.

The doctrinaire, high-art Modernists of the '30s were none too happy with the results of this extensive federal subsidizing of architecture. Frederick A. Gutheim, writing in the July 1940 *Magazine of Art,* effectively summed up their reservations when he wrote, "The entire building program has not produced one architectural masterpiece." Since Gutheim's interest was the merchandising of his version of the modern, i.e., the International Style, his criticism of most of these buildings as being, at best, "half modern" was valid.[63] But like other apologists for the International Style—both then and now—he was a bit confused as to what architecture is really about and to whom it is symbolically directed. The buildings to which he referred, in L.A. and elsewhere, were oriented to a middle-class audience that expected a traditional, "modern" (with its implications of the future), and utilitarian product; and the federally funded buildings of the '30s were, in fact, reasonably successful in providing this mixed imagery. L.A.'s large-scale public buildings (built or projected) were, like so many other federal buildings of the '30s, an exquisite expression of monumental P.W.A. Moderne, or

as some critics have labeled them, "Fascist Moderne."

Those Angelenos who believed in expressing the primacy of the traditional urban core had an ongoing dream of a monumental Classical civic center.[64] Since the teens, L.A.'s civic leaders and architects had been pressing for a "City Beautiful" County and City Administration Center. Other than the building of the Los Angeles City Hall in 1926-28, not much had actually been done except to prepare reams of sophisticated Beaux Arts drawings. But the urge to create such a symbolic center was renewed with great vigor in the late 1930s. William H. Schuchardt of the Los Angeles City Planning Commission wrote: "When the Civic Center of Los Angeles has been sufficiently completed, some years hence, to produce an effect of monumentality, it will be the most impressive group of city buildings in the whole country."[65]

In 1939 seven of the "establishment" members of the Southern California Chapter of the American Institute of Architects formed a committee, under the direction of Sumner Spaulding, to work on the design for the new Civic Center.[66] Their design, submitted in 1941, but never realized because of the war, visualized a handsome and, indeed, impressive Beaux Arts cross-axial scheme. The buildings, which were intended to line a great open mall, were, like the already completed Federal Building, to incorporate "new inventions and new methods of construction, and yet . . . be on guard lest they be led astray into fields removed from long established laws of composition."[67] The laws referred to were, of course, those of Classical Beaux Arts composition. By stripping away excessive historical detail, relying on simple rectangular volumes, smooth surfaces, and square fluted piers instead of columns, Sumner Spaulding and his colleagues showed how closely in touch they were to the stripped Neoclassical designs of Germany, Italy, and elsewhere. Equally close in spirit was Stiles O. Clements' U.S. Naval and Marine Corps Armory of 1939-40, whose forbidding exterior would have been very much at home in Berlin in the late '30s.

A miniaturization of the architectural styling of the proposed L.A. Civic Center was built by the city of Long Beach as its Civic Center. Side by side, facing an open square, were placed three public buildings, which, while hardly awe-inspiring, were still Classical and monumental. The most Classical of the group was the Veterans Memorial Building (George W. Kahrs, 1936) with its eagle sculptural frieze by Merrell Gage; the most Moderne was the Municipal Utilities Building (c. 1937-38).[68]

In quality of design the two most successful of the smaller city halls built in the L.A. area were the Santa Monica City Hall of 1938-39 (Donald B. Parkinson and J.M. Estep), and that designed by William Allen and W. George Lutzi for Burbank (1940-41). Though of reinforced concrete, the Burbank City Hall was detailed so that its mixture of classical P.W.A. Moderne and Streamline Moderne reads as a finely assembled machine product. Its lightness, even delicacy, is reinforced by the relief and free-standing sculpture of Bartolo Mako. The Santa Monica City Hall, with its low, horizontal-louvered tower, poses equally as a machine object—in its case as a delightfully enlarged Streamline Moderne home appliance.

Stripped Classicism (aptly labeled later as "P.W.A. Moderne") was a favorite of the Post Office Department even before the Depression, and the L.A. Basin abounds in examples ranging from the 1933 Hollywood Post Office (Claud Beelman and John E. and David C. Allison) to the smaller, less monumental Santa Monica Post Office of 1937 (Neal A. Melick and Dennis Murray). In a few instances, the Classical styling was more Mediterranean, as in Ralph C. Flewelling's beautifully proportioned Beverly Hills Post Office of 1933. The solidity of Classicism provided an appropriate vault-like setting for the Los Angeles Branch of the Federal Reserve (John and Donald B. Parkinson, 1930-32).

Other public buildings, with purposes generally thought of as more utilitarian, often discarded the Classical and fully embraced the Streamline Moderne. The Pan-Pacific Auditorium (Charles F. Plummer, Walter Wurdeman, and Welton Becket, 1935), which was built for the National Housing Exposition, remains a popular, much-admired classic of the new style.[69] Sumner Spaulding and John C. Austin's proposed curved, two-story glass-façaded main terminal for the L.A. Airport (1941) was a highly successful pre-World War II version of the academic Modernism of the 1950s. More typical of the styling of these utilitarian buildings was the small fire station, Fire Company No. 1, in East Los Angeles (1940). Its fins, band windows, horizontal grooves, and projections make it a classic example of the Streamline Moderne.

Stripped Classicism—P.W.A. Moderne—became, in the L.A. area, synonymous with the use of exposed concrete. In John C. Austin and Frederic M. Ashley's steel and concrete Griffith Park Observatory and Planetarium (1935), the concrete surfaces symbolized traditional masonry construction.[70] Far to the east, in San Dimas, the Metropolitan Water District's Water Softening Plant (Daniel A. Elliott, 1939-40) used rough boards and plywood to give character to the poured concrete surfaces of the "modified Spanish Colonial" building.[71]

Stripped Classicism, usually with an admix of Streamline Moderne, occurred in an impressive way in several of L.A.'s principal flood control projects of the 1930s. While both the Sepulveda and the Hansen Flood Control Dams in the San Fernando Valley were of the earth-filled type, their spillways and control towers were of reinforced concrete.[72] Like Hoover (Boulder) Dam on the Colorado River, the central concrete portions of these two dams beautifully illustrate how fully the Streamline Moderne expressed the image of present and futuristic technology.

Of all governmental constructions in the L.A. area (and in California as a whole), public school buildings were the most original and inventive in design.[73] Because of earthquake-resistance standards, school buildings were generally of reinforced concrete, and most revealed the patterns of the form boards on their exterior surfaces. The ideal of the open-air school, which, in California, goes back to before 1910, was increasingly used even in the more conservative and monumental schools. The styling of the buildings ranged from the outright Streamline Moderne of Thomas Jefferson High School in Los Angeles (Morgan, Walls and Clements; Styles O. Clements, 1936) to the more reserved Moderne of Mark Keppel High School in Alhambra (Keith Marston and Edgar Maybury, 1939). Occasionally there appeared suggestions of the Pre-Columbian, such as occurred in the two-story window panels of Hollywood High School (Norman Marsh, David Smith, and Herbert Powell, 1934 and 1938). In a few rare instances a suggestion of the Mission or the Spanish Colonial Revival was mixed with the Moderne, as in John E. and David C. Allison's Santa Ana High School of 1936-37.

As 1940 approached, there was a general tendency in these Southern California school buildings to discard the monumental and to suggest something much lighter and more fragile. The concave front of the Lou Henry Hoover School in Whittier (William H. Harrison, 1938), with its thin band of relief sculpture, suggests the delicacy of Hollywood Regency; and, with a careful selection of details, the Long Beach Polytechnic High School (Hugh R. Davies, 1934-36) could qualify as an example of the pre-World War II International Style. The only pure examples of L.A. area schools that fully expressed the International Style were Neutra's 1935 Corona Avenue School in Bell and his 1938 Emerson Junior High School in West Los Angeles. In both designs Neutra carried on and refined the earlier California tradition of the open-air school.

A look into L.A. at the end of 1939, illustrates that the Moderne was by no matter of means the only image for L.A.'s public buildings. For example, Mount Saint Mary's College in Brentwood Heights (M.L. Barker and G. Lawrence Ott, 1938-39) was Spanish Gothic; the projected sanctuary of Our Lady of Guadalupe in East Los Angeles (Henry Carleton Newton, 1939) was Mexican Churrigueresque; and the First Baptist Church of Hollywood (Douglas McLellan and Allen McGill, 1935) was of the "Formal Georgian type."[74] Ralph C. Flewelling's Post Office in Beverly Hills (1933) was a chaste Northern Italian Renaissance building. (Flewelling, nevertheless, followed his successful Beverly Hills Post Office with his own traditional, yet innovative, version of the classical P.W.A. Moderne in his 1939 Architecture and Fine Arts Building and Fisher Art Gallery at the University of Southern California.) And one of the largest public buildings in L.A., the 1938 Los Angeles Union Passenger Terminal, which was to receive the new streamline trains, lightly harked back to the Spanish Revival '20s with its arches, towers, courtyards, and tile.[75] The architect Paul Hunter remarked at the time of the ceremonial opening of the station: "Certainly, I know of no other city in which the arriving passengers leave the station through an open patio, filled with bright flowers and shady pepper trees, and flanked by tall palms. This scheme undoubtedly originated with local publicity men, but they have certainly hit upon an ideal introduction to Southern California."[76]

Despite these exceptions, the major stylistic shift of the '30s to the Moderne (and, in a few instances, to International Style) packaging of public buildings represented a major change from the Spanish Colonial Revival, which had been the style for schools and county/city buildings during the '20s.

Governmental public art—murals, sculpture, and mosaics—was viewed as a necessity for public buildings, and, like other American urban centers, by the end of the decade, L.A. could boast of a fair amount of public art.[77] This public art was a serious art meant to inspire, to promote faith in the American way, in American history, in the virtue of work, and in the ultimate victory of science and technology.

As often happens with an art that makes a high pretense to seriousness, much of the P.W.A. art ended up being lamentable to the high-arters of the '30s and humorous to us today. Technically most of the paintings, reliefs, and three-dimensional sculptures were reasonably competent, but few of them were executed by artists of real talent. Even with these limitations, however, the works expressed a freshness and optimism, even a sense of childlike naivete. They easily took their place in the design of the buildings with which they were associated and substantially contributed to the overall effect of those buildings.

Mildly modern didactic murals and sculpture had been widely used throughout the U.S. by government and business during the '20s.[78] The '30s simply carried on this tradition, with the federal government, through the Federal Art Project and other agencies, becoming the major patron. There was a certain shift of emphasis that can be detected in this public art of the '30s. While technology and the future were still strongly extolled, there was an increasing hint of nationalistic nostalgia for the virtues of America's past.

In L.A. as elsewhere, the great Mexican muralists, Rivera, Orozco, and Siqueiros, were highly influential. All three of these artists worked in the Los Angeles area during the '30s. Orozco painted *Prometheus* at Pomona College, and Siqueiros taught at Chouinard Art Institute and painted an outdoor mural in the courtyard of the school.[79] Generally, local L.A. muralists borrowed certain stylistic mannerisms from the Mexican artists, but they almost always ignored or played down any Marxist social content. A rare exception for L.A. was the episode of the painter Leo Katz. In 1937 Katz produced several panels for the Frank Wiggins Trade School that stepped just a tiny bit out-of-bounds in their implied criticism of American business and capitalism, and they were "quite understandably" removed.[80] But this "regrettable" incident was minor; most of the painters and sculptors followed the straight and narrow, glorifying episodes of America's past or pointing with open enthusiasm to the new technology of the future.

Another error the artists of the '30s generally avoided was communicating their message in too "elitist" a style. Stanton McDonald-Wright painted a series of panels for the Santa Monica Public Library on "the cinema," and in 1941 Grace Clements painted a series for the Long Beach Airport Terminal, both of which could be considered as the nonrepresentational "extreme," although both were readable.[81] Much more typical were Hugo Ballin's eight wall murals representing *The March of Science Through the Ages* inside the Griffith Observatory (1934-35), the murals of Edward Biberman in the Federal Building depicting events in Los Angeles history, and Buckley Mac-Gurrin's 1935 *Gastronomy Through the Ages,* appropriately placed in the cafeteria of the Los Angeles County Museum of History, Science and Art in Exposition Park.[82]

Compared to the previous decade there were few large private business buildings constructed in L.A. that could contain sculpture and murals. Business structures, nevertheless, continued to utilize art. The largest new downtown building built in the '30s, the Sunkist Building, boasted two sets of murals by Frank Bowers and Arthur Prunier, which appropriately used the orange as their theme.[83] The 1934 Streamline Moderne State Mutual Building by William Richards had murals by Millard Sheets in the Directors' Room and exterior relief sculpture by S. Cartaino

Scarpitto.[84] The rotunda of the Los Angeles Times Building was enhanced with a series of didactic murals by Hugo Ballin. They depicted the glories and civic contributions of the metropolitan press.[85] The new rage for photomurals was well on its way, and Will Connell and Edward Weston, among others, provided them for numerous Hollywood and West L.A. professional and industrial offices.[86]

Sculpture in all forms, particularly relief sculpture cast in concrete, was a must in almost every public building. George Stanley's three large-scale programmatic pieces for the Hollywood Bowl—a kneeling woman to symbolize music, an 11-foot male to symbolize drama, and an 11-foot female to symbolize dance—became a major tourist attraction. Westlake Park (now MacArthur Park) was the site of Nina Saemundsson's 1935 *Prometheus,* an eight-foot cast black male figure; and Harold Wilson's nude female figure, emerging from its fountained pool, was located at the entrance to the Ambassador Hotel on Wilshire Boulevard. These works were more obscure in subject matter than most public art, and their message was primarily that "modern" art can lend a high tone to a commercial or civic project.[87]

Schools were a favored place for programmatic relief sculpture, for there no red-blooded American could possibly argue that art should not be used to elevate and instruct. The long relief panel over the main exterior frescoes at the entrance to the Lou Henry Hoover School in Whittier presented the *Pageant of Education* by Bartolo Mako. On the walls of the Manual Arts Building of Redondo Union High School (John B. and David C. Allison, 1931) an airplane, the cogs of a machine, and a mechanic's tools proclaimed this as a place to prepare the young for the new industrial world. Above the entrance to the Science Building of Hollywood High School (1934-35) an exterior relief by Bartolo Mako depicts—like the then-popular radio serials—great moments in the history of science.

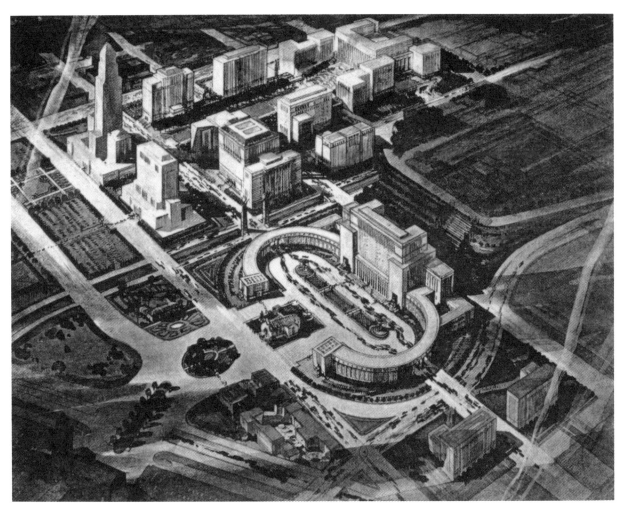

91. Project: Los Angeles Civic Center
Sumner Spaulding
1939

92. Project: Los Angeles Civic Center
Sumner Spaulding
1939

93. Veterans Memorial Building
George W. Kahrs; sculpture: Merrell
Gage
Long Beach, 1936

94. Federal Building
G. Stanley Underwood
Los Angeles, 1938-40

95. Post Office Building
Claud Beelman; John E. and
David C. Allison
Hollywood, 1935

96. Post Office Building
Ralph C. Flewelling
Beverly Hills, 1933

97. Burbank City Hall
   William Allen and W. George Lutzi
1941

98. U.S. Naval and Marine Corps Armory
Stiles O. Clements
Los Angeles, 1939-40

99. Los Angeles Union Passenger Terminal
John and Donald B. Parkinson and Herman
Sachs; landscaping: Tommy Tompson
1938

100. Project: Airline Terminal, Los Angeles Airport
Sumner Spaulding and John C. Austin
1940-41

101. Fire Company No. 1
Los Angeles, 1940

102. South Pasadena High School
     Auditorium
     Norman Marsh, David Smith,
     and Herbert Powell; sculpture:
     Merrell Gage
     1935-36

103. Henry E. Huntington School
     Norman Marsh, David Smith,
     and Herbert Powell
     San Marino, 1936

104. Emerson Junior High School
     Richard J. Neutra
     Los Angeles, 1938

104

105. Thomas Jefferson High School
     Morgan, Walls and Clements; Stiles O. Clements
     Los Angeles, 1936

106. Hollywood High School, Science Building
     Norman Marsh, David Smith, and Herbert Powell;
     drum relief sculpture: Merrell Gage: relief sculpture
     on building: Bartolo Mako
     1934-35

107. Lou Henry Hoover School
     William H. Harrison; sculpture: Bartolo Mako
     Whittier, 1938

106

108. Hayfield Pumping Plant
     Architectural Department, Metropolitan
     Water District
     35 miles east of Indio, 1936

109. Hansen Flood Control Dam
     San Fernando Valley, 1940

110. *Early California*
     Stainless steel and enamel relief
     sculpture for Mark Keppel High School
     Millard Sheets
     Alhambra, 1939

111. Mosaic for Long Beach Airport Terminal
     Grace Clements
     1941

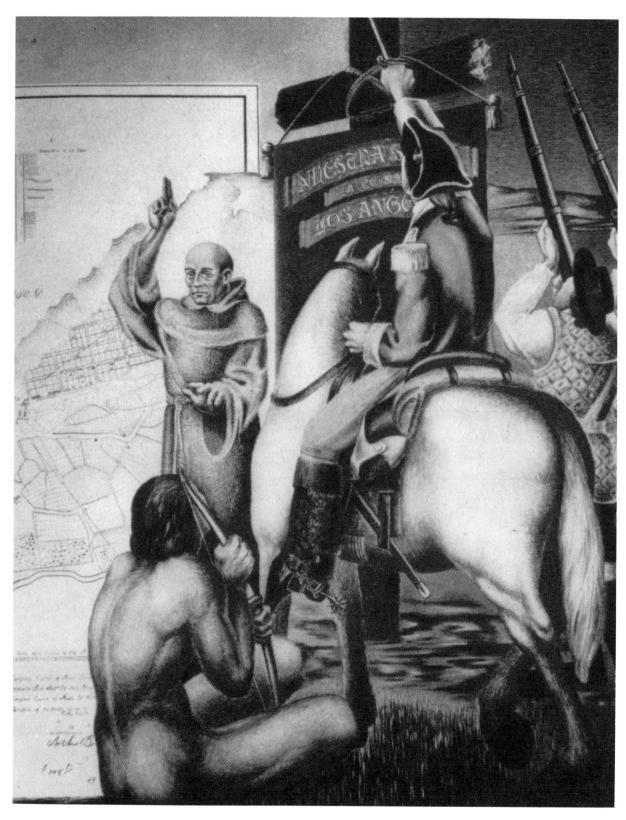

112. *Early 19th Century California*
Mural for the Federal Building
Edward Biberman
Los Angeles, 1940

RESIDENTIAL

On July 23, 1932, the Museum of Modern Art's exhibition "Modern Architecture" was presented on the fifth floor of Bullock's Wilshire. Among those who were members of the Honorary Committee sponsoring the exhibition were Gordon B. Kaufmann, H.C. Chambers, and Sumner Spaulding, three establishment figures of the Southern California Chapter of the American Institute of Architects. Richard J. Neutra, the only Californian included in the exhibition, certainly hoped that the it would not only further his own career, but would advance high-art Modernism.

One senses that Kaufmann, Chambers, and Spaulding (and, in general, the public who, visited the exhibition), responded to it as imagery, essentially devoid of its theoretical and social connotations. The forms of high-art Modern architecture were a new, exotic—essentially European—image, which could compete with, but not replace the already existing set of traditional images then in fashion. Like "Technocracy," another supposedly rational and scientific Southern California product of the early '30s, high-art Modern architecture was, for most Angelenos, something to flirt with, to enjoy, but in the end, not to take too seriously as ideology.

By the end of the decade, it was evident that the easy-going mood of traditional architectural images, made them more rational (i.e., responsive to the specifics of environment and to the needs of their occupants) than the more puritanical, insistent forms of Modernism. By 1941 the give and take between Modernism and traditionalism in Los Angeles domestic architecture in the '30s produced a set of modernized traditional images and, on the opposite side of the ledger, a set of traditionalized Modern forms.

Neither the city nor the county of Los Angeles became involved in low-cost multiple housing until late in 1937, when the Congress passed, and President Roosevelt signed, the Lanham Act creating the U.S. Housing Authority. With passage of this act, direct federal funding was made available. Later in 1937 the Los Angeles Housing Authority applied for financing to build Ramona Gardens, the first of the city's low-cost housing projects. Between 1938 and late 1941, Los Angeles built 12 public housing projects.[88]

As with public low-cost housing elsewhere in the U.S., costs for these projects were kept at rock-bottom, and the stinginess of expenditures openly advertised that this was housing for that regrettable segment of the population that had not made it. Both Ramona Gardens (1938-40) and Aliso Village (1941-42) brought together a talented group of designers including Lloyd Wright.[89] But even their combined design ability could not maneuver the available land and the construction costs to create really amiable environments. Probably the most successful in this regard were two smaller low-cost projects, Lake City and Estrada Courts, which were designed between 1939 and 1941 by Robert E. Alexander. However, all these low-cost housing projects did exhibit several decided advantages over those built elsewhere in the U.S. High-rise never entered the picture; the units were all one- and two-story, suggesting the image of the freestanding, single-family residence. They carried on the L.A. tradition of the wood-framed, stucco-sheathed box, and the dullness and repetition of the structures was usually quickly hidden by fast-growing vegetation.

Two little known, but fascinating, Los Angeles-area housing projects of the mid-'30s were spon-

93

sored by the Department of Interior, Division of Subsistence Homesteads. In these projects—one in El Monte, the other in the San Fernando Valley—the Federal Government provided funding for the erection of 50 small single-family houses in each locale.[90] Seventeen different plans for these "Rurban" homestead houses were developed by Joseph Weston. The image employed was that of the Colonial or California Ranch House; in cost, each dwelling ranged from $2,500 to $4,000 (including three-quarters of an acre of land). Loans were provided at $4.20 per $1,000 a month over a 30-year period.

As early as 1939, the local housing authority, working with the federal government, began to orient some of the low-cost projects toward defense housing. Typical of these was the 300-unit Harbor Hills Project on the hillside above San Pedro. Harbor Hills was laid out by New York planner Clarence S. Stein, and the buildings were designed by an L.A. team headed by Reginald D. Johnson.[91]

Between 1941 and 1942 seven more large-scale projects were built, the most renowned of which was Richard J. Neutra's Channel Heights Project.[92] The budget for these war-time workers' housing projects was substantially more than had been made available for the earlier public housing. The impressive hillside site above San Pedro where the Channel Heights housing was situated enjoyed a panoramic view of the Pacific and was more than ample in size. By preserving the basic contour of the site and the deep eucalyptus-covered arroyos, Neutra was able to suggest suburbia, rather than the typical urban housing project. The buildings themselves—some two-story, some one-story—were stylistically less doctrinaire and insistent than his usual work of these years. The exterior surfaces and detailing of the exposed wood structure were sensitively contrasted against white stucco walls; and the shed and gable roofs placed the buildings even closer to the middle-class ideal of domestic architecture.

The '30s also saw a scattering of private projects that sought to provide, perhaps not low-cost, but at least inexpensive, multiple housing.[93] The first of these was Wyvernwood (David Witmer and Loyall F. Watson, 1938-39) located off Olympic Boulevard at 8th Street. The most renowned was Baldwin Hills Village (Reginald D. Johnson, Robert E. Alexander, and others, 1941).[94] The architecture of the one- and two-story Baldwin Hills Village units was kept simple and low key. What

made it work, in contrast to the usual federally funded projects, was the ample size of its site, its site layout (by Reginald D. Johnson), its lush landscaping (by Fred Barlow, Jr. and Fred Edmonson), and the larger budget available for each unit. With the intensified need for housing defense workers at the end of the '30s, private developers were encouraged to build "spec" housing near aircraft and other defense industries. Again, it was Neutra, in his Victory Gardens in North Hollywood, who went beyond the usual barracks-like stucco boxes.

Though private developers and builders could not match the number of new multiple housing units provided in public low-cost and war-time housing projects, they did construct an amazing number of middle-middle and upper-middle-class units between 1937 and 1942. The largest of these was the Park La Brea Apartments just off Wilshire Boulevard and Fairfax Avenue (Leonard Schultze and Associates and E.T. Heitschmidt, 1941-42). Park La Brea, built by Metropolitan Life Insurance Co., was an Easterner's version of life in L.A.

More characteristic of Los Angeles were the many smaller, locally financed, developer projects, such as View Park and the earlier Olympic Village. Some of these housing units were duplexes and four-plexes; others like the 196-unit Aetna Housing Project (W. George Lutzi, 1941), at Crenshaw Boulevard and Slauson Avenue in Southwest L.A., were on a much larger scale.[95] Certain districts and boulevards were favored locales for the more expensive upper-middle-class multiple housing. These included the area just south of Wilshire Boulevard in Beverly Hills; Wilshire Boulevard itself, east of Westwood Village; and parts of Los Feliz Boulevard.

Most of this private housing loosely carried on the bungalow court/garden apartment approach of the 1920s. Those projects, consisting of four or more units, were U- or L-shaped and oriented around one or more garden spaces. Often garage units were placed directly adjacent to the street with the living units above and behind.[96] All were constructed with a wood frame sheathed with stucco, and were only rarely over two stories high. One or more garage spaces per apartment were provided. Even in the moderately priced Aetna Project there were 162 garage spaces for 192 units.

The usual architectural imagery of these multiple units was the Hollywood Regency, which was a mild mixture of Eastern Colonial, two-story

Monterey, and Streamline Moderne. Off the drawing board of Paul R. Williams, Walter Wurdeman and Welton Becket, Myron Hunt and H.C. Chambers, and others, came numerous garden apartments suggesting this or that historic tradition, but they were always functionally modern in plan and even Streamline Moderne in detailing—in their use of curved walls, glass brick, and portholes. Some designers, such as Milton J. Black, narrowed their imagery to one mode—in his case to the Streamline Moderne. In the end, though, these garden apartments were all quite similar in siting, in provision for out-of-doors living space, and in plan.

Exceptions to the dominance of the Streamline Moderne and period styles were the few private multiple housing units designed by L.A.'s avant-garde Modernists. As in the '20s, L.A.'s small contingent of high-art Modernists carried on their intense ideological battle against their "misguided" opponents, the traditionalists. "Real Modernity," wrote Schindler in 1935, "is not a question of a different set of cornices and columns, but is based on a new attitude toward life and its frame, the building."[97] But the architect William Orr Ludlow answered Schindler's argument by pointing out that ". . . what is fundamentally wrong is the theory on which these [Modern] houses are designed, which comes from supposing that people act according to reason, while the fact is that reason just brings us facts and sentiment makes the decision."[98]

Notably unsentimental in image, Neutra's eight-unit Strathmore Apartments (1939) were in the pure International Style. Although located on a steep hillside lot, they were sited like the earlier bungalow courts of the '20s. His 1939 Landfair Apartments also showed a full commitment to the International Style in their horizontal bands of windows, machinelike white stucco walls, and flat roofs and roof gardens.

R.M. Schindler designed over a dozen apartments and duplexes during the decade. Of these, three were built, a good average for him: a duplex for Mrs. Mackey (1939), an apartment complex for Bubeshko on Griffith Park Boulevard (1939 and 1941), and an apartment complex for Falk (1939). All these structures were functionally and visually as complex as Neutra's appeared to be simple, rational, and direct. The Mackey duplex, located on a flat West L.A. site, consisted of a two-and-one-half-story stucco box with secondary volumes projecting out of it. The Bubeshko apartments climbed like steps up a hillside. The Falk apartments, occupying an almost impossible building site, were designed to be read only in fragments, not as a whole.

Like Schindler and Neutra, other L.A. avant-gardists used the International Style, but worked out new variations of the bungalow court/garden apartment in their designs. Ain did this in his 1937 Dunsmuir Apartments in which he created a narrow walkway entrance on one side of the lot so that a modest sized terrace and garden were available on the other side. Davidson's 1940 Drucker Apartments in Brentwood enclosed a walled garden. Compared with those units clothed in Streamline Moderne or historic imagery, the avant-gardists' designs seem radical and different, but a closer look at their siting, plans, structure and materials, concern for out-of-doors living, and commitment to the automobile reveals their similarities to the mainstream.

But even with multiple housing units on the increase, the detached single-family dwelling was still the structure that really counted for most Angelenos. The '30s marked a high point (only equaled during the same decade in the Bay region to the north), not only for the often advertised models of modern architecture, but also for those houses that expressed historic imagery.

National and regional competitions, sponsored by home shelter and professional magazines, by the producers of building products, and by national and regional housing organizations had, by the 1920s, become very much a part of the architectural scene. Along side these competitions for single-family housing were the continual sponsorships of model or ideal houses. The adverse effects of the Depression of the '30s encouraged an increase in both competitions and the construction of model houses; and the general lack of commissions prompted older established architects as well as younger professionals to enter these competitions and to participate in various projects for model houses.

In the '30s national competitions sponsored by Better Homes in America, by magazines such as the *Architectural Forum, Life,* and *House Beautiful,* the General Electric Company, the Monolith Portland Cement Company, and others were repeatedly won by Los Angeles architects. H. Roy Kelley and Winchton L. Risley won gold medals in the competitions held by the Washington-based Better Homes in America; and Roland E. Coate, H. Palmer Sabin, Ralph C. Flewelling, and H. Roy Kelley placed high on the awards lists of other national competitions.

Regionally, in California, one of the most revealing signs of changing architectural taste was the Hundred Year House Competition of the Simons Brick Company of Los Angeles.[99] Edgar F. Bissantz's winning scheme was formal, almost Hollywood Regency; H. Scott Gerity adapted the Regency mode to a completely circular house; and H. Roy Kelley colonialized the California Ranch House.

The two largest housing exhibitions held in Los Angeles during the '30s were the 1935 National Housing Exposition and the 1936 California House and Garden Exhibition. The former had as its centerpiece the Pan-Pacific Auditorium. The California House and Garden Exposition occupied much of the 5900 block of Wilshire Boulevard.

In addition to the Pan-Pacific Auditorium, the outdoor exhibits at the National Housing Exposition included three demonstration homes, among them the "House of Tomorrow," sponsored by the *Los Angeles Times* (designed by H. Roy Kelley, Edgar Bissantz, and Harold G. Spielman; landscape architecture by Katherine Bashford). This demonstration house was accompanied by "The Village of Tomorrow," which consisted of 27 small-scale models of houses. Within an auditorium, symbolizing the essential link of water and power to the city's horizontal spread of single-family houses, was a large-scale model of Gordon B. Kaufmann's Power House for Hoover (Boulder) Dam.

For the California House and Garden Exposition of the following year, six houses were built, and these ran a broad gamut including a Modernist plywood house by Richard J. Neutra, a New Orleans cottage by John Byers and Edla Muir, an English Cottage by H. Roy Kelley, and a French Cottage by Paul R. Williams. Marie Louise Schmidt, who organized the exhibition for the Architects Building Materials Exhibit, cast the whole production in the manner associated with a preview of a new '30s Hollywood film; and it was all highly successful in the local and national attention it drew and in the number of visitors.

In addition to these housing expositions with their demonstration houses, many other individual model houses were also built. For example, the Los Angeles Home Planning Bureau sponsored a close-to-unbelievable remodeling of a 19th century Queen Anne Cottage into an Anglo-Colonial Cottage. In West Los Angeles, developers such as the Janss Corporation and the Westwood Mortgage and Investment Co. built, on a yearly basis, a series of individual demonstration houses.

From the '30s to the present, a strong influence on architecture and design has been attributed to the Hollywood film, a view summed up very clearly by Neutra in 1941:

> Motion pictures have undoubtedly confused architectural tastes. They may be blamed for many phenomena in this landscape such as: Half-timber England peasant cottages, French provincial and "mission-bell" type adobes, Arabian minarets, Georgian mansions on 50 by 120 foot lots with "Mexican Ranchos" adjoining them on sites of the same size. A Cape Cod fisherman's hut (far from the beach and fish) appears side by side with a realtor's office seemingly built by Hopi Indians.[100]

On the surface this view of the Hollywood film as a design precursor seems convincing, and it would appear to be reinforced by the actual participation of several major designers, such as Lloyd Wright and Kem Weber, in the design of film sets.[101] A careful look, however, at the products of the Hollywood film industry during the '20s and '30s, ranging from Gloria Swanson's *What a Widow* (1930) to Fred Astaire and Ginger Roger's *Shall We Dance?* (1936), shows that the architecture depicted in these films solidified current taste rather than leading the way.[102] Sets were derived from the real world of Hollywood and Beverly Hills, not the other way around. Even the cities of the future that science fiction films placed before the viewer were restrained and behind the times.[103] It seems, therefore, that Neutra and other apologists for elitist high-art architecture were using "low-art" film as a convenient scapegoat.

Though varied traditional images were used by L.A.'s architects of the '30s, their work easily reads as a single tradition. The Regency, the Colonial, the Tudor, the French Provincial, the Spanish, or the Monterey were loosely fashioned to create the atmosphere of a particular moment of the past. But the illusions were always gentle and not persistent, and they were carefully tied functionally and symbolically to the present. Low-scaled volume, bland uninterrupted surfaces, easy-going, rationally devised plans, and an ability to open up to the out of doors, did as much to establish the real mood of these houses as did their historic illusions.

As occurred elsewhere in the country, the enthusiasm for the Anglo-American Colonial, with its hidden, or openly declared, nationalistic overtones, played with a number of late 17th through early-19th century forms. In Southern California the general preference was for what was labeled at the time the "Colonial Farmhouse type." Around the middle of the '30s this Colonial type turned towards the stone Pennsylvania Colonial type found in the work of Gerald R. Colcord, H. Roy Kelley, and John Byers and Edla Muir. By the end of the decade the refinement and simplicity of American Federal (often called "Regency") seemed close to the Moderne, without abandoning references to the past.

America's and Southern California's changes in taste from the '20s to the '30s is closely mirrored in the suburban houses lived in by Hollywood film stars, directors, and producers. The fashionable architectural image for the silent film stars of the '20s was that of the Mediterranean and Spanish; in the '30s the pendulum of taste swung over almost completely to versions of the Anglo-American Colonial. Brian Donlevy, Claudette Colbert, and Andy Devine settled on the pine-paneled New England Colonial. Fred MacMurray and Richard Dix ensconced themselves within stone Pennsylvania Colonial homes; Jane Withers, Dick Powell, and Francis Farmer selected Colonialized California Ranch Houses; and David O. Selznick, Sam Goldwyn, Margaret Lindsay, and Dorothy Lamour commissioned Colonial designs that absorbed many features derived from the Moderne.

Sunset, in a 1941 article, "Successful Transplants," captured the intensity and enthusiasm for the Colonial image: "Mr. and Mrs. Robert Taylor (Barbara Stanwyck) made several trips to Williamsburg to record colored movies of the features they liked about the restoration and spent much time collecting authentic furniture before building their home in San Marino."[104] Joe M. Estep's 1939 design for Richard Dix's Beverly Hills house was described as: "Big, substantial, comfortable, unassuming . . . the handsome Pennsylvania Colonial stone residence . . . is in character with its owner whose historic portrayals of rugged pioneers of the old west so truly reflect the man himself."[105]

The Anglo-Colonial image was a persistent one in numerous speculative housing developments in Los Angeles in the late 1930s. The landscape architect A.E. Hanson in his design and development of Rolling Hills atop the Palos Verde Peninsula had Paul R. Williams and Lutah Maria Riggs create Williamsburg-inspired Colonial houses for his Williamsburg Lane.[106] "To the north in the San Fernando Valley, Alan Stearns commissioned his architect Arthur Herberger, Jr. to design his residence as a 'New England Village,' including the Gate Keeper's house as a replica of a Connecticut Church, and the garage as a copy of a New England fire-engine house."[107]

Paul R. Williams' Tyrone Power house of 1937 and his Jay Paley house of 1938 show how period architects selected historic fragments, then carefully arranged them as elements upon a modern, logically functional building. A driveway entrance façade might be "correct" in its Georgian or Regency proportions and details, but the generally plain walls, the lowness of the building to the ground, and the almost universal horizontality of these designs were "modern."

During the '20s, along with the Spanish and Mediterranean, the favored French image for single- and multiple-family housing was the French Norman farmhouse; in the '30s the tendency was to abandon this rural vernacular source, and look to the smaller, more formal 18th century French manor houses and pavilions. Often the French qualities of high pitched (or even Mansard) roofs were mixed with elements taken from the English Regency. Such a combination occurred in Roland E. Coate's 1932 house in Beverly Hills for Richard B. Gudgor—a dwelling that won both regional and national awards. In the '30s, however, the general approach to the French Provincial image was to treat it as a single-floor dwelling that was formal in its composition and highly refined in its details. Roland E. Coate realized these classical ideals in several San Marino, Pasadena, and West Los Angeles houses, the Ruppel house of 1938, in San Marino, being an excellent example. Lutah Maria Riggs also looked to this French source for the image of her 1935 Leon Graves house in Van Nuys, with its walled entrance court defined by a gatehouse and guest quarters, together with a formal axial entrance leading to the house.

It was the young architect John E. Woolf, however, who really ended up setting the stage for the popularity of this image after World War II.[108] Woolf's trademark was over-scaled, paired entrance doors and steeply pitched Mansard roofs, often surmounted by classical sculpture or finials. The style eventually became a trademark for L.A.'s physical image, much as the Mission and Mediterranean/Spanish styles had earlier typified the city.

John W. Byers and Edla Muir, in their 1936 house for the parents of Shirley Temple, tastefully used historic odds and ends to mirror a version of the past that never existed: medieval English chimneys and dormers; a round tower topped by a French Provincial weathervane; double-hung, shuttered windows, placed low in a stone-veneered wall (perhaps an allusion to Pennsylvania Colonial); and a make-believe windmill suggesting a medieval fairytale.

Though there was a dramatic drop in the total number of spec houses built in Los Angeles after 1931, 56 of those built, the Spanish or Mediterranean image continued to prevail. By the mid- to late-'30s, when building activities were on the increase, the Anglo-American "Cape Cod" cottage became increasingly popular (as it did throughout the country). In an advertisement of 1940, the West-Side Village Company presented its Cape Cod model, ". . . the most popular and permanent designs in all American architecture."[109] The $2,990 plan for a single-floor Cape Cod retained some Colonial flavor, but at the same time it could assume the guise of a California Ranch House, or that of a Bermudian dwelling with Federal/Regency overtones.

When the Mediterranean/Spanish was employed for larger-scale houses in the '30s it, like the Colonial, was increasingly abstracted, and Moderne details were often added. Myron Hunt and H.C. Chambers' large-scale house for Dr. O.C. Welbourn in Encino (1940) was of Spanish design. (It included a separate three-story mirador, a chapel, and a Moorish garden.) All of the fenestration and details, however, were so simplified that its volumes and surfaces come close to the Moderne.[110]

By the early '30s, the two-story porched Monterey dwelling had replaced the Spanish Colonial Revival as the fashionable style.[111] H. Roy Kelley, Roland E. Coate, Donald MacMurray, and Palmer Sabin increasingly "colonialized" the original 1830s and 1840s historic prototype with 18th century windows, doors, and fireplaces. In some instances they designed the cantilevered second-story balconies of elaborate wrought iron, and thus transformed the design into what was considered "New Orleans" style. These '30s Monterey dwellings were well-publicized in the home shelter magazines and professional journals, and they were even built in the Midwest and the East. The Monterey style was seen as part of the national Colonial style, as something that was regional to the West, and, at the same time,

houses in the style were modern in plan and in their openness to the out of doors.

Roland E. Coate, Palmer Sabin, Ralph C. Flewelling, and H. Roy Kelley often designed in the Spanish Monterey style, and in the single-story California Ranch House style, both of which lent themselves beautifully to symbolizing California's Hispanic past and to expressing the emerging modernism of the '30s. These same designers did equally well with other historic images: Anglo-Colonial, English, or French Provincial. Sumner Spaulding, Douglas Honnold, and George Russell preferred the Regency, generally mixed with an occasional swatch of Streamline Moderne. The resulting houses tended to be sophisticated and refined, hinting at the taste expected in an upper-middle-class environment.

Even the largest of these '30s period houses was smaller and more intimate in scale than their counterparts in the '20s. Such reduction in scale (but not necessarily in actual size) was a basic stylistic ingredient of the '30s; the ship's cabin provided imagery not only for the Modern and the Moderne, but also for the period architects.

The plans of these houses were seldom impressive as two-dimensional drawings, but they indicate that the architect and client sought designs that would be easy and functional to live in. Interior movement was effectively handled, generally by a communications center, off of which were situated the entrance, living and dining spaces, kitchen, stairs, and a lavatory. Wide openings, usually groups of French doors, led out from downstairs rooms to adjoining covered porches and outdoor living spaces. The driveway, parking area, and garage—all oriented to the automobile—usually provided the major means of entering the house. If a walkway happened to lead from the house to the street, it was of secondary importance.

Out of this gentle use of the past emerged one of the major housing forms of this century, the California Ranch House. Looking back into California's architectural tradition, it is apparent that the ranch house developed in the '30s was an updated version of that other great California export, the California bungalow of the early 1900s. It was, of course, much more as well, for like the larger period house of the decade, it insisted on an element of historicism and was both highly functional and simple in volume, surface, and details. Its plan approached perfection for the needs of its time. It allowed an informal spread of one interior space into another, an openness to the out of doors (usually away from the public street), and a loving accommodation of the automobile.

Though Southern California is often considered the home of the California Ranch House of the late '30s and on, it should be remembered that the style emerged simultaneously in the Bay region. As the editors of Sunset magazine observed in 1937: "The California Ranch House Style is widely and deservedly stylish at present."[112] Still, if one individual can be credited with its invention, it was the gifted L.A. designer Cliff May.[113] His single-floor, informal ranch houses closely hugged the ground and created intimate interior spaces. They were almost universally referred to at the time as "charming" and, without being overly sentimental, they were indeed. The style enhanced the anti-urban image so important to suburbanites of the '30s. May's ability to retain the romantic sentiment of the past and to encompass the modern can be seen in his meandering, single-floor "Lily Pond" hacienda (1936-37), and his more modernized interpretation for his own "Rancheria" in Mandeville Canyon (1936), which had interior furniture by Paul T. Frankl.

The theme of the ranch house, almost always colonialized and modernized, was popularized by many other Los Angeles architects and designers of the decade: Whitney R. Smith, Garrett Van Pelt, Harold O. Sexsmith, Palmer Sabin, Eugene Weston, Jr., Roland E. Coate, H. Roy Kelley, and Sylvanus Marston and Edgar Maybury. By late 1941 the image of the ranch house was fully taken up by the spec builders, and it was increasingly the vogue for larger-scale, single-family housing projects in West Los Angeles and in the San Fernando Valley.

Though the number of Modern and Moderne houses built in L.A. in the '30s was modest, especially when compared to historically inclined products, there was still no other region of the country which was as open to the imagery of the "new." As already indicated, this renaissance of the Modern and the Moderne was due to the increasingly healthy condition of L.A.'s economy in the later '30s coupled with a clientele that desired the image of the way-out. Finally L.A. provided the architectural talent to carry it off. A rich variety of compositions filled the pages of California Arts and Architecture and Architect and Engineer. Dominated by one figure, Richard J. Neutra, domestic architecture ran the gamut from the complex spatial compositions of R.M. Schindler to several of the country's most suave exponents of the Streamline Moderne. In between these ends

of the scale were such important talents as J.R. Davidson, Paul Laszlo, Raphael Soriano, Gregory Ain, and Harwell H. Harris. The view that the Modern and Moderne of these years constituted a renaissance was sensed locally and was equally apparent nationally.[114]

The dividing line between the Modern/Moderne and period architecture tended, as has been indicated, to be very fuzzy. The well-established residential architects of L.A. produced numerous houses with many earmarks of the Moderne—curved walls, glass bricks, corner windows, and portholes worked into relatively plain, stucco-sheathed boxes. These houses tended to be open, with increased attention placed on relating usable, out-of-doors living space to the interior. They proved to be highly liveable environments and remained within L.A.'s stucco-box tradition.

A bit more far-out were the purely Streamline Moderne houses of the L.A. area, most of which were designed by younger architects, who are often little-known today, and by contractor/builders. A few of these are real modern classics, like the Maharajah of Indore's house in Santa Ana (Donald Beach Kirby, 1939) or any one of the Los Feliz and West Los Angeles houses by Wesley Eager, Edgar Bissantz, Adrian Wilson, Milton J. Black, or Robert Derrah. Modest Moderne project houses were scattered hither and yon from Long Beach to the San Fernando Valley. A few were built as groups, such as those in Easterly Terrace in the Silverlake district (William Kesling, 1935-38), but most were built as one of a kind "come-on" products to bring prospective buyers out to a new subdivision.

Another group of designers, including Jock Detlof Peters, Paul Laszlo, and Kem Weber, occupied a position a step closer to the accepted canons of the International Style (i.e., the doctrinal Modern). Though all were Europeans (and European trained), they quickly acclimated themselves to California, and while some of their work occasionally has a European flavor, it could never have been built anywhere except California.

Peters' Sheppard house in San Marino (1933) smacks of the European or East Coast Moderne except for its outrageously large round window; his Gilks house (1933) in Hollywood, with its numerous usable balconies and secluded exterior living space, came quite close to the '30s designs of Neutra and Schindler.[115]

Peters also designed for developer William Lingenbrink, an insistent patron of the Modern and the Moderne. At the end of the '20s Lingenbrink projected a retreat for writers, artists, and others, which he called "Park Moderne." The retreat was located in the then-remote reaches of the San Fernando Valley (in present-day Calabasas). Lingenbrink required that all of the buildings and houses in the retreat "be along modern lines." Peters designed the retreat's Community Building (1931), and in the early '30s, he and R.M. Schindler were commissioned to design several model "lodges" for it.[116]

Paul Laszlo, like Weber and several others, labeled himself an industrial designer rather than an architect. Shortly after arriving in Los Angeles in 1937, he designed a cantilevered hillside house dominated by a curved glass-walled living room and accompanying balcony. Though his design for this projected house suggests the nautical, i.e., a ship's bridge, it was formalized by his European experience to be first a Modern art object and only secondarily nautical and Streamline Moderne. The following year Laszlo built a more straight-forward house for his own use, which was typically California Modern on the outside, while the interior swayed between the purity of the International Style and his own version of a more luxurious and posh "Hollywood" Modern. Though he devoted a good share of his time in the '30s to interior decorating and the design of furniture, Laszlo produced a fascinating group of residences in the decade. Some were outright Moderne; others, like the Blanke ranch house (1942) in the San Fernando Valley, fall completely within the tradition of the California Ranch House.[117]

Like Laszlo, Kem Weber also devoted much of his creative energy to the design of furniture and other industrial products, and to teaching.[118] His realized houses of the '30s, such as the Wedemeyer house in Altadena (1937) and his Gisler house in Glendale (1942-43), are lukewarm Moderne. His most interesting architectural designs occurred right at the end of the period, when he, along with just about every L.A. architect (part of a nationwide phenomenon), became involved in prefabrication for defense housing. Although only a trial model was built, his plywood defense housing shows how he had completely thrown off not only his European predilections, but also his attachment to the Streamline Moderne in favor of a full-fledged "modern" California Ranch House.

The one designer in the '30s who most elegantly brought the European Modern and California styles together was J.R. Davidson. He also catalogued himself at first as an industrial designer, later as an architect. His first designs of the late '20s and early '30s were commercial, but by the mid-'30s he increasingly turned his attention to domestic architecture. His Stothart (Phillips) house in Santa Monica (1937-38) and his later house for the writer Thomas Mann in Pacific Palisades (1941) handsomely sum up the ideal pre-World War II Modern house.[119] They are solid and substantial in feeling and are factually and symbolically functional.

The major maverick of the L.A. Modern scene was Rudolph M. Schindler. As Henry-Russell Hitchcock remarked in 1938, he just did not fit comfortably into any conventional pigeonholes.[120] Within the European and American Modern movements a legion of architects have professed a deep overriding concern for interior space. But, excepting Frank Lloyd Wright and Lloyd Wright, the realized space of both the Moderne and Modern tended to be limited to horizontally layered space. In contrast, Schindler's houses of the '30s aptly show his desire to design a complicated series of internal vertical and horizontal spaces and to express these internal spatial changes externally through projecting and receding volumes.

Schindler's highly personal version of space and its expression had little or no influence nationally, although his designs did inspire the younger L.A. designers Gregory Ain and William Alexander (originally known as Alexander Levy).[121] The Schindler houses that received the widest publicity were those approaching the International Style. His Buck house of 1934, the Rodakiewicz house of 1937, and his dramatic, hillside Van Patten and Walker houses (1934-35 and 1935-36, respectively) were well illustrated in architectural journals and popular home magazines, including the Home Section of the *Los Angeles Times*. The photographs selected to illustrate these houses expressed their most dramatic Modern aspects, never their other qualities.

With space and volume his major concern, Schindler's approach to styling in this decade was highly varied. At the beginning of the '30s he still felt that the Modern was closely married to concrete. His schemes for small, low-cost dwellings, such as the Schindler Shelter (1932-34), are like fragments of post-Cubist sculpture. His projected Locke house (1933), by curving concrete surfaces into one another, suggests the image of an industrial product.

By the mid-'30s Schindler adopted some elements of the Streamline Moderne, ranging from curved wall and roof surfaces to portholes, glass brick, and built-in and free-standing furniture, which verge on the Hollywood Moderne. Then, in keeping with changing fashion, his work began to be less Modern and more openly informal and woodsy. His A-frame Bennati cabin (1934-35) located at Lake Arrowhead, goes back to earlier A-frames he designed in the '20s. His Southall house (1938) was one of the earliest all-plywood houses in L.A. His final pre-World War II houses, like the Dekker house in Woodland Hills or the Rodriguez house in Glendale (both 1940) illustrate the relaxed, less stringent version of Modern architecture that began to emerge after 1935. By 1940, Schindler had abandoned any reference to the machine as a dominant expressive image in his houses.

Neutra followed a similar course, from the machine as the visual symbol for the house, to the machine more implied than stated. But Neutra, in contrast to Schindler, never abandoned his goal of symbolizing the rational and objective in his houses. The industrial image persisted, elegantly, in all of his work during the '30s. Sometimes he expressed this image through the combination of steel, glass, and stucco (his own Research house, 1933); through steel alone (Beard house, Altadena, 1935); or through the suggestion of prefabrication in his plywood houses (Plywood Experimental house, 1936).

Neutra, too, played with the Streamline Moderne in his projected Modern Steel Craft house (1934), his Sten-Franke house in Santa Monica (1936-38), and in that great classic streamlined steel ship, the Von Sternberg house in the San Fernando Valley (1936). But, like Schindler, the sense of the Streamline never overpowered his designs.

The same is true for Neutra's more woodsy houses of the late '30s and early '40s. The small redwood-sheathed McIntosh house in Los Angeles (1939) is simply one of his earlier stucco boxes beautifully sheathed in wood; the 1942 Nesbitt house in Brentwood Park went a step farther toward woodsy warmth by its use of brick floors and walls with cement mortar oozing from the joints. But when Neutra employed materials popularly thought of as traditional, he used them rationally for their tactile quality—they were a surfacing material that mellowed the machine image, but did not compromise it.

By the mid-'30s, Davidson, Schindler, and Neutra had been joined by Harwell H. Harris, Gregory Ain, and Raphael Soriano. All three had been associated with Neutra: Harris had worked in his office from 1930 until 1933, Ain from 1932 until 1935, and Soriano in 1932.[122]

Of the three, Soriano emerged as the strongest Modern purist, the one who worked most faithfully within the stylistic confines of the International Style. Such Soriano houses as the Kimpson-Nixon house in Long Beach (1939) or the Lukens house in Los Angeles (1940) are even more "correct" versions of the International Style Modern than Neutra's work of the period. Occasionally Soriano admitted other elements— a bit of streamlining as in the curved living room of the Lipetz house (1935), or the slightly mellowing atmosphere of wood sheathing in the courtyard-oriented Strauss-Lewis house (1940)—but his aim always remained to express a machine Spartanism. An editor wrote of one of his 1940 interiors: "The austere simplicity . . . is conducive to relaxation and study."[123]

The '30s buildings of Gregory Ain were very different from those of his mentor, Neutra, or his contemporary, Soriano. In 1943, in a commentary for a Designs for Post-War Living Competition sponsored by *California Arts and Architecture,* he wrote:

> Instead of acknowledging standardization and prefabrication as the incidental means to economical mass production of good dwellings, we have almost made prefabrication an ultimate aim in itself. And after having attacked blind subservience to tradition, we finally evolved an almost equally blind tolerance for any suggestion of tradition, regardless of intrinsic merit.[124]

He went on to argue that Modern architecture should produce the "machine for living," but that there was no necessity to symbolize this machine imagery in the product. If we look at Ain's houses of the '30s it is apparent that, though he basically followed this dictum, he had, of necessity, to clothe his buildings in some sort of stylistic imagery, and his imagery was naturally related to what other Southern California Modern architects were doing. Thus certain interior and exterior aspects of his 1936 Edwards house and his 1937 Ernest house (both in Los Angeles) are Schindleresque, though their carefully laid out plans are not. By the early '40s he, too, was designing loosely spread-out houses, like the Domela house in Los Angeles (1942), which are closely related to the California Ranch House. Not accidentally, Ain's houses came close at times to the contractor/builder houses of the period, since his concern for a small-scale, functional environment, which could be realized by using existing building technology, brought the two moderately close together. This is well illustrated in the Daniels and Tierman houses in Los Angeles (1937 and 1939), which used the box as a basic form and modulated the space within and also, in part, without.

The third member of the young Modernists, Harwell H. Harris, headed in a different direction. Harris' early projects of the late '20s and early '30s were classical Modern, and although he abandoned this "correct" Modern quite early, it cropped up mixed with Streamline Moderne as late as 1937 in the Santa Monica Canyon house of John Entenza, who was later to become the editor of *California Arts and Architecture.* Of the younger L.A. designers Harris was the first to look back at California's own tradition—in his case to the woodsy bungalows of the Pasadena architects Charles and Henry Greene. Like the Greenes, he also looked to Japan for inspiration. In his Lowe house in Altadena, designed with Carl Anderson (1934), he arrived at one of the most handsome plans devised for a suburban house. Its courtyard-oriented plan was Hispanic, but its neutral, anonymous wood-sheathed exterior, covered by a low, hipped roof, was essentially Japanese in spirit. Even more openly committed to the Japanese was his own house in Fellowship Park, Los Angeles (1936), but in it he gave a nod to Schindler, who in the '20s had used sliding screens in a somewhat similar fashion. By 1936 Harris was combining these Japanese elements with vertical and horizontal spaces and details reminiscent of Frank Lloyd Wright's Usonian house of those years. Harris' most successful fusion of these elements—the Japanese, Wright's Usonian schemes, and Neutra's Modernism—occurred in his Birtcher-Share house in Los Angeles (1942).

Frank Lloyd Wright himself was active in L.A., both as a visitor and lecturer and as a designer of several houses. His designs for these L.A. houses of the late '30s were decidedly more theatrical than his characteristic Eastern or Midwestern Usonian house.

His projected house for Arch Obler in Pacific Palisades, "Eagle Feather" (1939), seems to have been designed as a section of highway dramatically cantilevered out toward the ocean. Though clothed in traditional wood and brick, Wright's Sturges house in Brentwood Heights (1939) presses forth with all speed to sail out over West

L.A. Equally theatrical in its interplanetary sense of speed were several other of Wright's West Coast projects of the late '30s, including his unrealized house for Arch Obler (1940), which was to have been perched atop the mountains above Malibu. Though much of Wright's work from the mid-'30s reflected his fascination with the drama of the Streamline Moderne, his West Coast designs seem the most insistent of all in their Buck Roger's quality. Was it the agitation and the open theatricality of the city or the competitive presence of other modern designers that pressed Wright into such dramatic statements?

Going in quite a different direction from the L.A. work of his father were the '30s designs of Lloyd Wright, whose work during these years was, on the surface, relatively calm and only marginally committed to the '30s modern image. In the mid-'30s he designed a number of residences, mostly for people in the movie industry, which were basically stripped period houses. Though generally restrained, these houses were anything but suave and polished; there were always very personal design elements that set them apart from the usual L.A. period houses of the time. In 1936 he designed his often illustrated Griffith ranch house in Canoga Park, which in its siting, plan, and spaces represents the perfect upper-middle-class suburban ranch house. In the late '30s Lloyd Wright followed the ranch house theme in several smaller versions. In all of these houses there occurred a sprinkling of his father's details. On occasion they even made reference to the elder Wright's plans. But Lloyd Wright's houses could never be mistaken for his father's.

At the end of the period, a new and younger contingent of designers began to come to the fore, and, by 1941, it could well be argued that modern architecture in L.A. had finally established itself as an ongoing tradition. The orientation of these younger men varied considerably. John Lautner, as a result of his long experience with Wright at the Taliesin Fellowship, brought along some of the master's stylistic baggage. His own house in the Silverlake district is lightly Wrightian, but his later Bell house in the Hollywood Hills (1940) and his Springer house in Elysian Park (1940) are closer to Harris than to Wright. A. Quincy Jones, who had worked in the '30s for Douglas Honnold and Paul R. Williams, cast his glance north to the Bay region when he designed his own studio-house in the Hollywood Hills (1938). Richard Lind, who had been with Schindler in the mid-'30s, and William Alexander simplified the older man's work in several really fine designs. Others, such as Thornton M. Abell, were determined to be Modern and generally pulled it off very well. Whitney R. Smith and Rodney Walker, two of the younger of the new designers, began to work out their own versions of the California Ranch House and, when World War II came, to suggest designs for prefabricated houses.

The indirect impact of the Depression on the practice of landscape architecture in the Los Angeles area was close to devastating. Several of the major landscape architects, such as Wilbur David Cook and George Gibbs, turned for employment to the National Park Service and the U.S. Forest Service.[125] Other prominent landscape architects, including Florence Yost, Ralph Cornell, Tommy Thompson, Katherine Bashford, Charles G. Adams, Edward Huntsman-Trout, Lucille Council, and Raymond E. Page, continued their residential practices only on a much reduced level.

As with the architects, many of the landscape architectural commissions came from the movie set. Sunset magazine noted in early 1938 that Tommy Thompson was ". . . putting the finishing touches on the gardens of Grace Moore, Robert Montgomery and Basil Rathbone."[126] The professional landscape architects were also prominent in the several housing exhibitions and model home projects of the '30s. Katherine Bashford provided the landscape design for the "House of Tomorrow" at the National Housing Exposition (1935), and Hammond Sadler, Charles G. Adams, Edward Huntsman-Trout, and Seymour Thomas designed the landscape for each of the six display houses at the 1936 California House and Garden Exposition.[127]

As a general rule, even in their smaller projects, the Los Angeles landscape architects of the '30s retained an element of formalism, i.e., a boxed garden or a central axis. But their major emphasis was to suggest informality and to provide usable terraces and covered pergolas and porches for easy-going, out-of-doors living. The post-World War II emblem of Los Angeles, the swimming pool, increasingly became an essential ingredient of the upper-middle-class garden.[128] In the realm of plant material, the tendency was to use fewer exotic "tropical" species and to employ trees and shrubs that seem to refer to Anglo-America, rather than to Hispanic America.

The design of furniture and interiors changed as rapidly during the '30s as did architecture. Traditional furniture and interiors continued to dominate the scene, but, like architecture, their designs underwent a strong simplifying process. Paul R. Williams took Regency and "Oriental" designs and made them modern, and Barker Brothers marketed a line of "Monterey" furniture that was closer in spirit to the then popular "Early American Maple" than to the Spanish Colonial Revival furniture of the '20s.[129]

Nostalgia for the West, certainly inspired by the Hollywood Western, was, in a way, a successor of the much earlier episode of California fumed oak, and of do-it-yourselfism. Sunset magazine illustrated many pieces of indoor and outdoor furniture that were Western in flavor. One of the most delightful was their "Covered Wagon Garden Seat." "Don't let the complicated appearance of the covered wagon fool you," wrote the editors of the magazine. "It's well within the hammer-and-saw school of carpentry."[130] But, even in the traditional house, there was a place for the out-and-out modern: chrome furniture for the dinette, or rattan for the den or the terrace. For those who were more bold, there were tables of glass brick, Lucite-covered desks, and curved plywood radio and phonograph cabinets.

Within this L.A. decorators' world of combed plywood and venetian blinds were a number of pre-eminent local and national stars. Kem Weber produced not only for the local scene, but also for Grand Rapids, the furniture capital of the United States.[131] Paul T. Frankl, who had already established a national reputation, abandoned New York and came to sunny Southern California. Paul Laszlo's show room on Rodeo Drive in Beverly Hills was a place of high fashion for the upper middle class.[132] Equally fashionable and impressively designed were the furniture of Hendrick Van Keppel and the textiles of Maria Kipp.[133] It was in 1940 that Van Keppel brought out his classic out-of-doors steel and cotton cord ottoman.

Though many of the avant-garde Modernists (especially Schindler) designed furniture in the '30s, most of their houses ended up containing Frankl or Laszlo tables and chairs—that is, if the clients could afford them. While period architects of this decade had no problem whatsoever in furnishing their houses with expensive or inexpensive traditional furniture, the Modernists were not so well served. If they wished to use furniture of good design, they had to fall back on architect-produced furniture (mostly simple, inexpensive plywood designs), or the costly designs of Frankl, Laszlo, Van Keppel, or Weber.

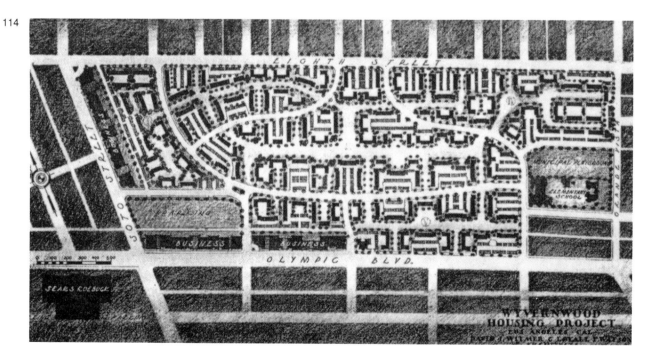

113. Wyvernwood Village
David J. Witmer and
Loyall F. Watson; land-
scape: Hammond Sadler
Los Angeles, 1938-39

114. Wyvernwood Village
Site map
Los Angeles, 1938-39

115. Baldwin Hills Village
Reginald D. Johnson,
Robert E. Alexander,
and others; landscape:
Fred Barlow, Jr., and
Fred Edmonson
Apartment interior
Los Angeles, 1941

116. Baldwin Hills Village
Community room
Los Angeles, 1941

117. Baldwin Hills Village
Site map
Los Angeles, 1941

115

116

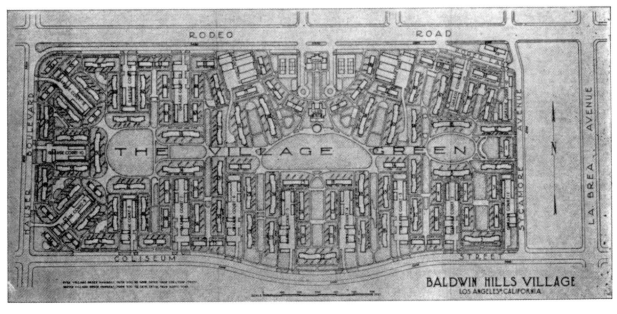

117

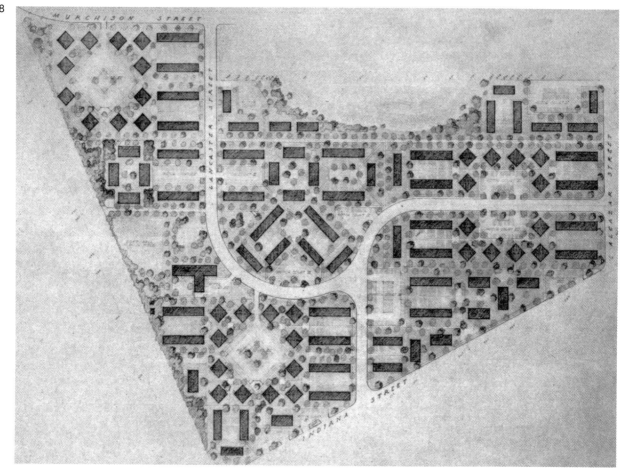

118.-120. Ramona Gardens
George J. Adams, Walter S. Davis, Ralph C.
Flewelling, Eugene Weston, Jr., Lewis Eugene
Wilson, and Lloyd Wright; landscape: Katherine
Bashford and Fred Barlow
Los Angeles, 1938-40

121

122

121. Aliso Village
George G. Adams, Walter S.
Davis, Ralph C. Flewelling,
Eugene Weston, and Lloyd
Wright; landscape: Katherine
Bashford and Fred Barlow, Jr.
Los Angeles, 1941-53

122. Subsistence Homesteads
Joseph Weston
El Monte, 1934

123.-124. Apartment building
Milton J. Black
Los Angeles, 1934

125

126

127

125. Strathmore Apartments
Richard J. Neutra
Los Angeles, 1937

126. Duplex for Mrs. Mackey
R.M. Schindler
Los Angeles, 1939

127. Bubeshko Apartments
R.M. Schindler
Los Angeles, 1941

128. Dunsmuir Apartments
Gregory Ain
Los Angeles, 1937

128

129. West-Side Village Company
     Spec Houses
     Los Angeles, 1940

Homes at Wholesale!

THE "COLONIAL"
2 Bedroom, House, Lot, Garage
Complete

$3490

$190
DOWN

EXCITING 1941 MODELS

ready for you to see... Homes shown here are just a few of many attractive designs for your selection ... only $190 down ... Complete with lot 53 to 61 feet in width!

HOW DO WE DO IT?

● We own the acreage. ● We plot the lots. ● We put in street improvements. ● We furnish the plans. ● We secure the permits. ● We buy in quantity. ● We buy wholesale. ● We keep our workmen steadily employed. ● We pour the foundation. ● We wire and plumb. ● We erect the dwelling. ● We arrange the finances ... No big commissions ... We sell direct.

● We deliver the deed with the keys to YOU in
ONE SINGLE OPERATION—from Acreage to Occupant!

$190
DOWN

NO PYRAMIDING of PRO

West-Side Village homes are constructed on an *efficient, scientific, waste elimin ating, money-saving plan.* . . .

Geared for volume production, pu chases of materials are made in car lo lots.

Lumber is loaded from ship-side and livered to our own material and assem yard on the property. Here it is pre-c master plan specifications; plum and electrical units are assembled. terial bundled, marked and deliver each home location.

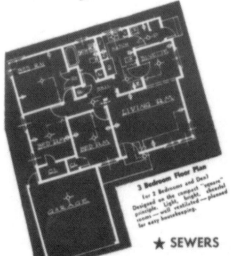

3 Bedroom Floor Plan
(or 2 Bedrooms and Den)
Designed on the compact "square" principle. Light, bright, cheerful rooms — well ventilated — planned for easy housekeeping.

★ SEWERS   ★ CURBS   ★ GUTTER

st·Side Village

LOCATION IDEAL *for Entire Family!*

For work . . . for school . . . for play. Surrounded by new homes West-Side Village is located in one of the MOST ACTIVE RESIDENTIAL AREAS in all Los Angeles. Just a few minutes' drive to Douglas Aircraft, Metro-Goldwyn-Mayer, Hal Roach, Selznick International and Fox-20th Century studios, Beverly Hills, U. C. L. A. and the beaches. *Climate is delightful* all year 'round. Transportation is excellent. *Schools, churches, stores and shops are* within easy walking distance. *Certainly* you will enjoy living in this congenial district of bright new homes, and friendly neighbors. . . .

—$3490.
2-BEDROOM HOUSE & LOT
All Improvements Paid

$29.90
MONTHLY

THINK it's SMART to be THRIFTY?

Don't let the low prices of West-Side Village homes lead you to think of *cheaply constructed houses on just so-so lots*. . . . You're due for a *pleasant surprise* when you see these homes. . . . Even if you CAN AFFORD to pay more money for a home you'll do well to see these two and three bedroom dwelling before you buy ANYWHERE at ANY PRICE!!

PLEASE be ADVISED . . .
Due to large government defense demands, conditions in the material market MAY NECESSITATE an IN-CREASE of PRICES QUOTED. . . . *We urge you to visit West-Side Village at once!*

"...MOUNT" No. 1 $4090
...ouse, Lot, Double Garage
Complete

...n WEST-SIDE VILLAGE

...it is handled by skilled workmen—
...one specializing in one *definite part*
...ome construction.

...d on Master Floor Plans carefully
...cted for their *Light, Ventilation, Con-*
...ience and *Easy Housekeeping Fea-*
...res these smartly-styled two and three
...droom dwellings offer the *Greatest*
...ome Values in Los Angeles today!

NO PLANS to BUY—NO FUSS—
NO BOTHER—NO WORRY
YOU SEE WHAT YOU'RE GETTING
BEFORE YOU BUY in WEST-SIDE
VILLAGE!!

$190 DOWN

"PARAMOUNT" No. 2 $4090
3 Bedroom House, Lot, Double Garage
Complete

LAST BLOCKS of Homes NOW SELLING . . . *Watch 'em GO!*

The instantaneous success of West-Side Village since its recent inception has attracted *National Attention and Comment*. . . . The completion of 776 homes marks the consummation of this Grand Scale Home Project . . . *The end is in sight*. With material prices on the up-swing and the increasing cost of land we *cannot expect to duplicate* these home values again. . . .

If you want a home at all we earnestly suggest that you get busy lest you *"miss the boat."*

● COME TODAY, TOMORROW or SUNDAY at the very latest!

★ PAVED STREETS   ★ DRIVEWAYS   ★ TREE PLANTING   ★ ALL INCLUDED IN OUR LOW PRICE ★

113

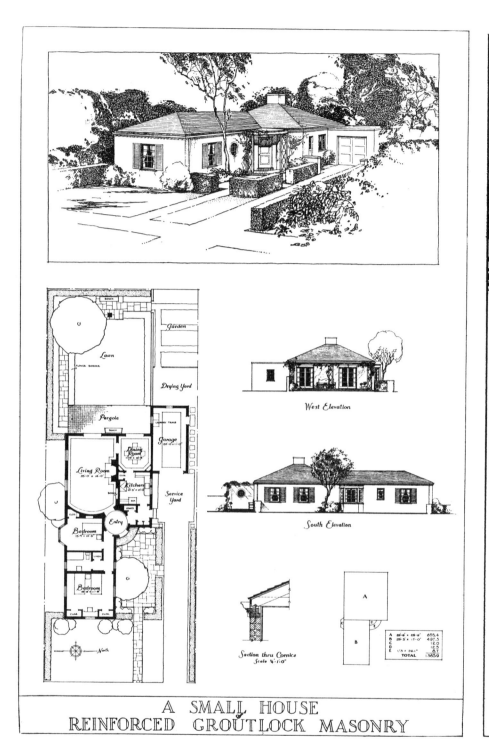

A SMALL HOUSE
REINFORCED GROUTLOCK MASONRY

A Small Ho
Groutlo

130. Hundred Year House
(Groutlock Masonry)
Competition
First prize design
Edgar F. Bissantz
Los Angeles, 1934

131. Hundred Year House
(Groutlock Masonry)
Competition
Honorable mention design
H. Roy Kelley
Los Angeles, 1934

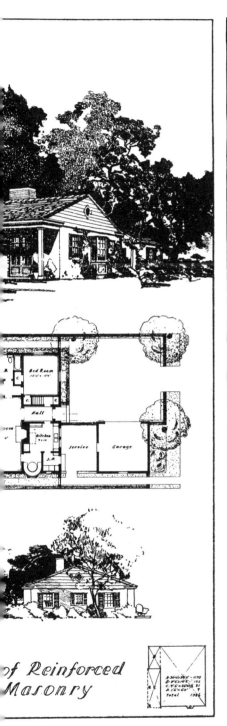

of Reinforced Masonry

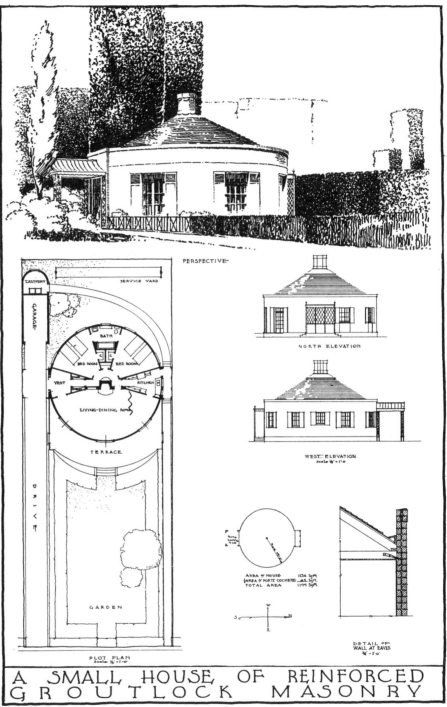

PERSPECTIVE

NORTH ELEVATION

WEST ELEVATION

PLOT PLAN

DETAIL OF WALL AT EAVES

A SMALL HOUSE OF REINFORCED
GROUTLOCK MASONRY

132. Hundred Year House
(Groutlock Masonry)
Competition
Honorable mention design
H. Scott Gerity
Los Angeles, 1934

133.-134. Project: Georgian house for
California
Edgar F. Bissantz
Los Angeles, 1935

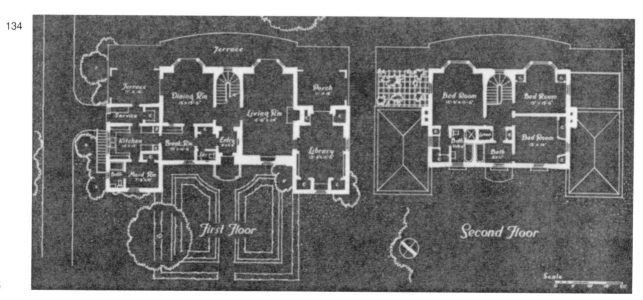

135.-136. Architectural Building
Material Exhibit: French house
Paul R. Williams
Los Angeles, 1936

137. Tyrone Power house
Paul R. Williams
Brentwood, 1939

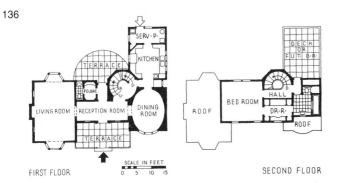

117

138

139

138. Haldeman house
     Wallace Neff
     Los Angeles, 1940

139. March house
     Wallace Neff
     Los Angeles, 1940

140. Ilsey house
     John Byers and
     Edla Muir
     Los Angeles, 1937

141. Chase house
     John Byers and
     Edla Muir
     Azusa, 1936

142. Forrest house
Roland E. Coate
Beverly Hills, 1933

143. O'Melveny house
Roland E. Coate
Bel Air, 1932

144. Davis house
    Roland E. Coate
    Pasadena, 1936

145. LeFens house
    Roland E. Coate
    Pasadena, 1933

146

147

146. Similey house
Roland E. Coate
Bel Air, 1933

147. Geis house
Roland E. Coate
San Marino,1937

148. Pringle house
H. Roy Kelley
Bel Air, 1936

149. Bugshaw house
H. Roy Kelley
Beverly Hills, 1938

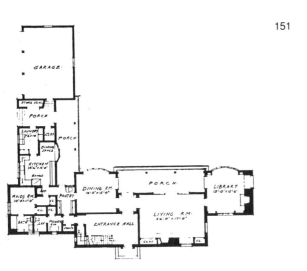

151

FIRST FLOOR PLAN

SECOND FLOOR PLAN

150.-151. Surber house
H. Roy Kelley
Rancho Santa Anita,
1937

152. Patterson house
H. Roy Kelley
Westwood, 1931

152

153. Hawks house
     Myron Hunt and H.C. Chambers
     Beverly Hills, 1936

154. Welbourn house
     Myron Hunt and H.C. Chambers
     Encino, 1940

155. Franck house
     Palmer Sabin
     San Marino, 1935

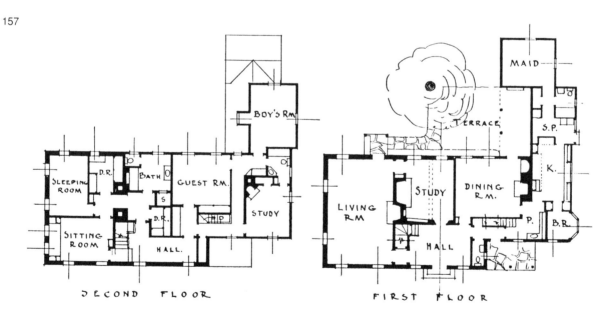

SECOND FLOOR

FIRST FLOOR

156.-157. Chambers house
Gerald R. Colcord
Beverly Hills, 1936

158.-159. Dick Powell house
Richard F. King
Toluca Lake, 1935

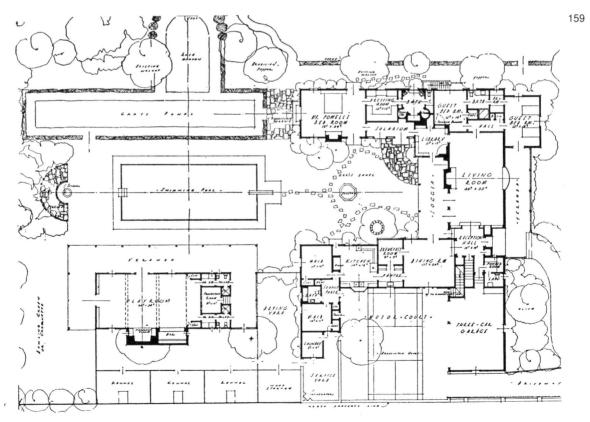

160

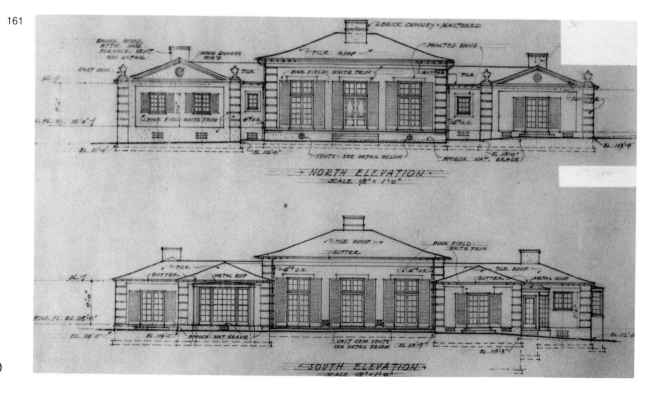

161

130

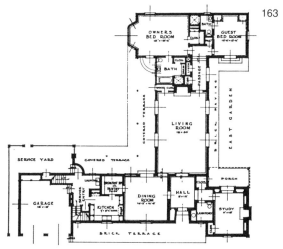

FIRST FLOOR PLAN
SCALE

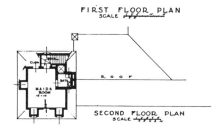

SECOND FLOOR PLAN
SCALE

160. Barbara Stanwyck–Robert Taylor
house
William D. Holdredge
San Marino, 1940

161. Graves house
Lutah Maria Riggs
Encino, 1935

162.-163. Fox house
Ralph C. Flewelling
Chapman Woods, Pasadena, 1932

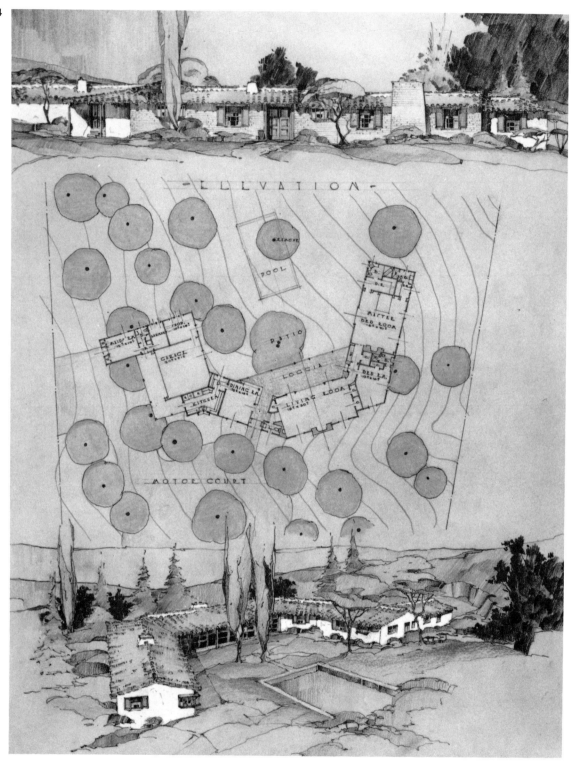

164. Project: "Alta Canyada" house
Cliff May
1938

165.-166. May house
Cliff May
Los Angeles, 1936

167

168

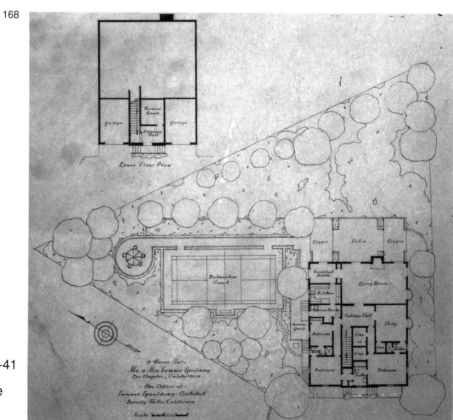

167. Project: Woolf house
     John E. Woolf
     Los Angeles, c. 1938-41

168.-169. Spaulding house
          Sumner Spaulding
          Los Angeles, 1937

170. Ulm house
   Milton J. Black
   Los Angeles, 1937

171.-172. Laszlo house
   Paul Laszlo
   Beverly Hills, 1937   137

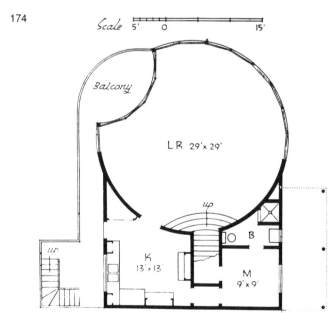

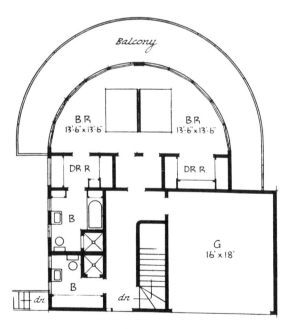

173.-174. Project: House
Paul Laszlo
Los Angeles, 1937

175. Harrison house
Paul Laszlo
Holmby Hills, 1940

176. Blanke ranch house
Paul Laszlo
San Fernando Valley, 1939

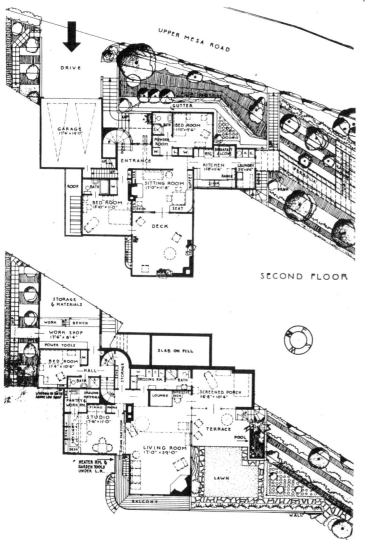

177.-178. Abell house
   Thornton M. Abell
   Santa Monica, 1937

179. Thomas Mann house
   J.R. Davidson
   Pacific Palisades, 1941

180.-181. Stothard house
J.R. Davidson
Santa Monica, 1938

182. Project: Franklin
house
Kem Weber
Los Angeles, 1938

183. Gisler house
Kem Weber
Glendale, 1942-43

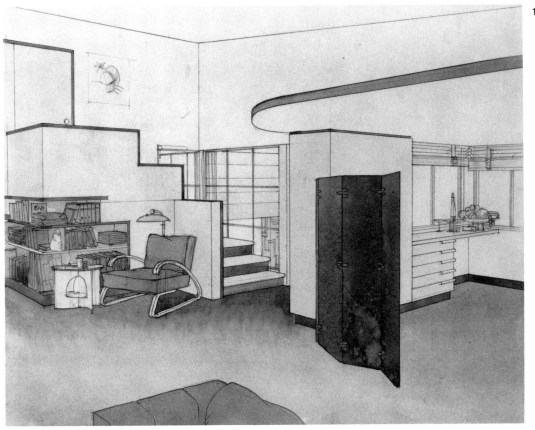

184

185

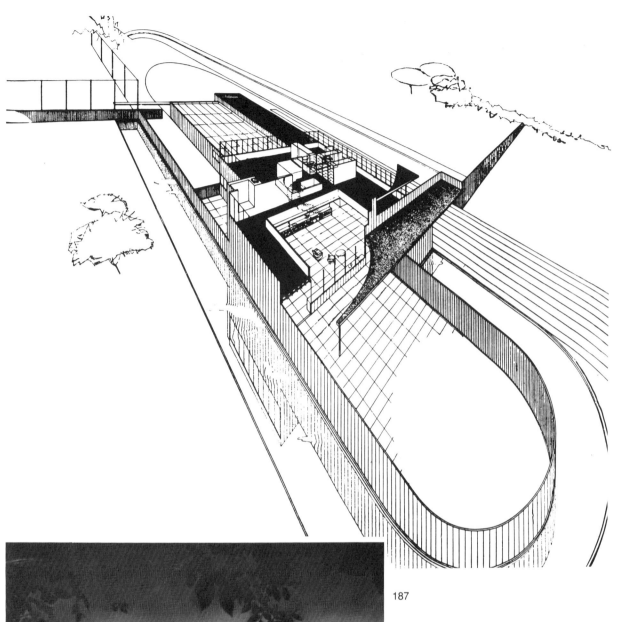

187

184.-185. Sten-Franke house
　　　　 Richard J. Neutra
　　　　 Santa Monica, 1934

186.-187. Von Sternberg house
　　　　 Richard J. Neutra
　　　　 Northridge, 1936

145

188

189

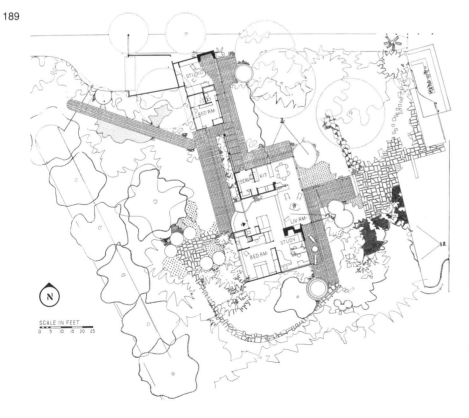

SCALE IN FEET
0 5 10 15 20 25

188.-190. Nesbitt house
         Richard J. Neutra
         Brentwood Park, 1942

191. Beard house
     Richard J. Neutra;
     Gregory Ain, associate
     Altadena, 1935

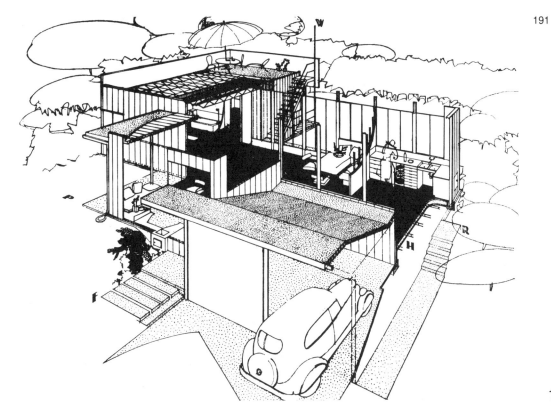

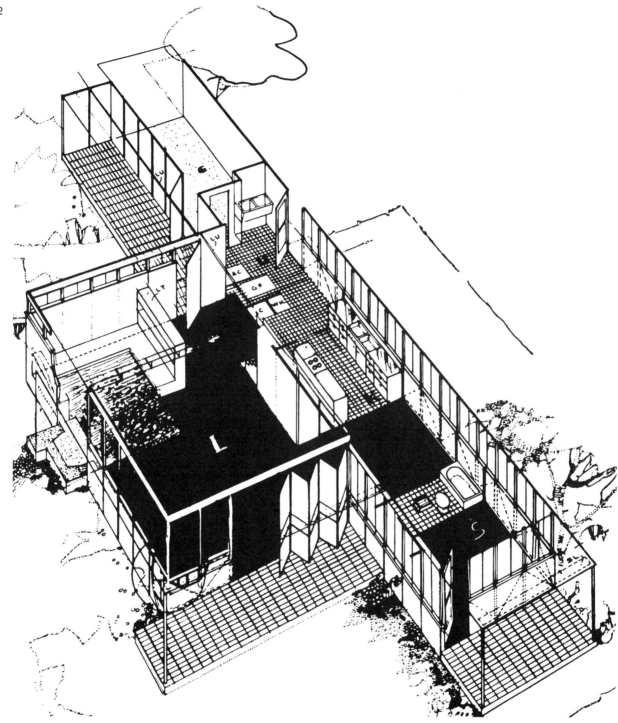

192. Plywood Model House
Richard J. Neutra
Los Angeles, 1936

193. Project: 4-1/2 Room Model
House (in concrete)
R.M. Schindler
Los Angeles, 1933

194. Rodriguez house
R.M. Schindler
Glendale, 1941

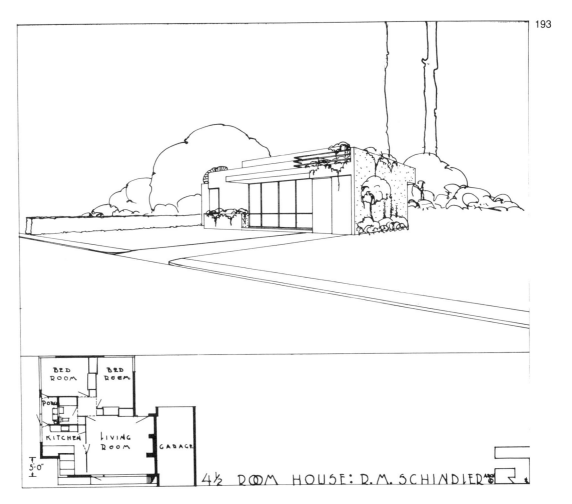

4½ ROOM HOUSE: R.M. SCHINDLER

195

196

195.-196. Van Patten house
R.M. Schindler
Los Angeles, 1934-35

197. Van Patten house
Living room with Schindler's
modular furniture

198. Harris house
R.M. Schindler
Los Angeles, 1942

199

200

202

199.-200. Strauss-Lewis
house
Raphael Soriano
Los Angeles, 1940

201. Nixon house
Raphael Soriano
Long Beach, 1939

202. Lipetz house
Raphael Soriano
Los Angeles, 1935

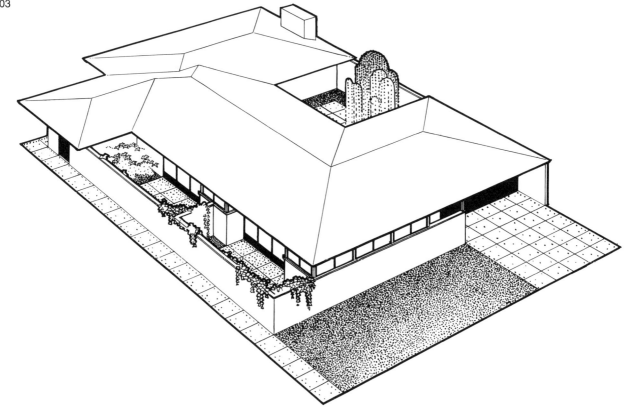

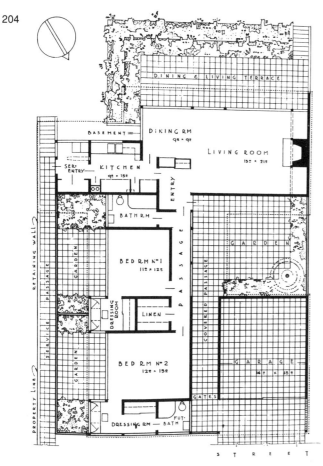

203.-204. Lowe house
Harwell H. Harris and
Carl Anderson
Altadena, 1933-34

205. Domela house
Gregory Ain
Los Angeles, 1942

206. Edwards house
Gregory Ain
Los Angeles, 1936

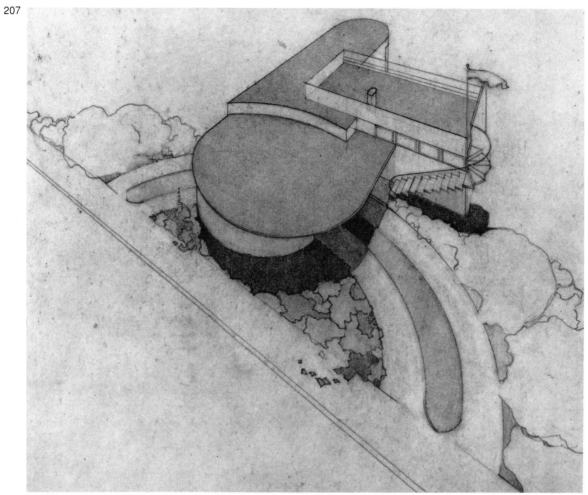

207

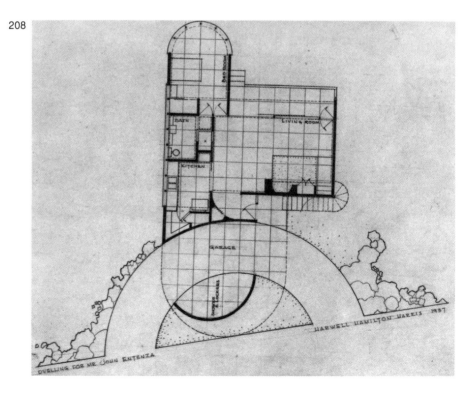

208

DWELLING FOR MR JOHN ENTENZA   HARWELL HAMILTON HARRIS 1937

207.- 208. Entenza house
        Harwell H. Harris
        Santa Monica Canyon, 1937

209. Project: House
        Harwell H. Harris
        Los Angeles, 1932

210. Birtcher-Share house
        Harwell H. Harris
        Los Angeles, 1941-42

209

210

211

212

213

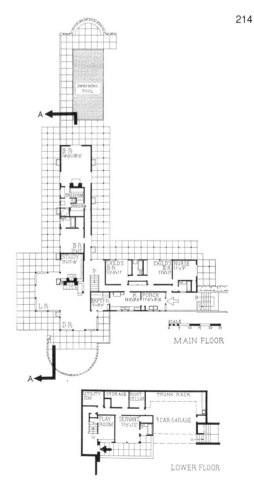

214

211. Hilliburton house
William Alexander (Alexander Levy)
Laguna Beach, 1937

212. House
Richard Lind
Los Angeles, 1939

213.-214. Griffith ranch house
Lloyd Wright
Canoga Park, 1936

159

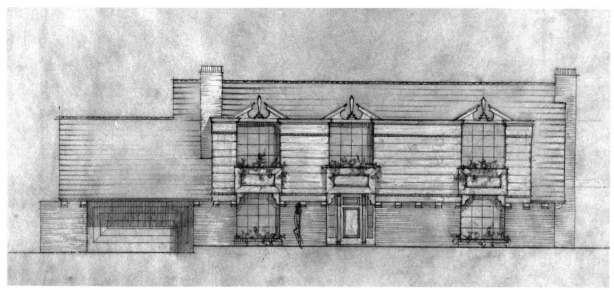

215. Project: Butterworth house
     (Scheme 1)
     Lloyd Wright
     Los Angeles, 1937

216. Project: Degener house
     Lloyd Wright
     Los Angeles, 1940

217. Project: Butterworth house
     (Scheme 2)
     Lloyd Wright
     Los Angeles, 1937

218. Lubsen house
     Lloyd Wright
     Altadena, 1940

219

220

219. Sturgis house
    Frank Lloyd Wright
    Brentwood, 1939

220. Project: Plyluminum House
    Whitney R. Smith
    Los Angeles, 1942

221. Covered-Wagon Garden Seat
    Editors of *Sunset*
    1938

222. Chair, ottoman, and radio side
    table for M. Shep
    R.M. Schindler
    1934-35

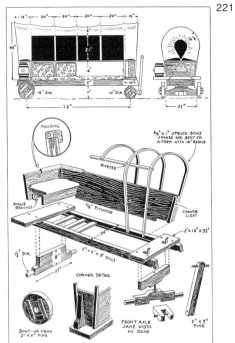

221

222

223. Furniture (in Laszlo Studio)
   Paul Laszlo
   Beverly Hills, 1940

224. Indoor/outdoor chair
   Paul Laszlo
   1940   165

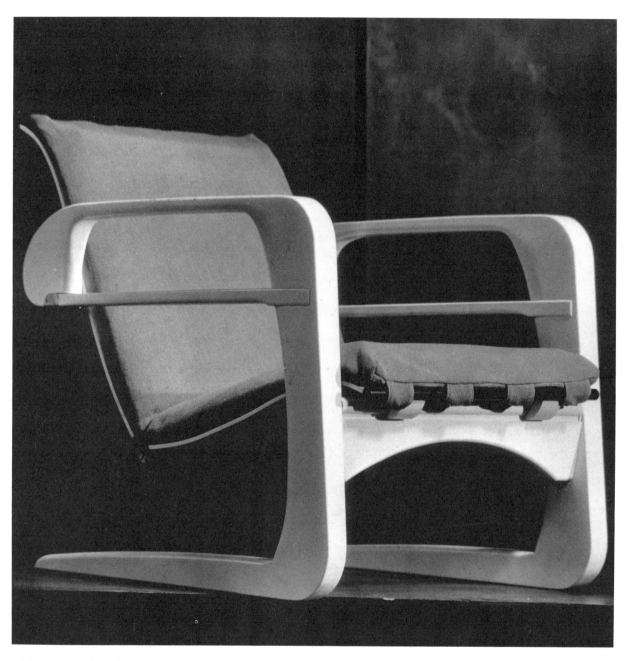

225. "Airline Chair"
Kem Weber
1934-35

1941

THE HIGH POINT OF architecture and design in the L.A. area occurred in 1939 and early 1940. The Depression, though still lingering on, seemed something of the past, and although World War II had started in Europe, it still seemed far removed. Before 1939, architecture and design had flourished, but after 1941 the new concern was defense. Thus the architecture and design scene in 1941 was markedly different from that existing in 1931.

The change was reflected not only in the architectural profession, which became increasingly committed in design and ideology to the Modern, but equally in those who packaged and presented the architectural and design world. In February 1941 John Entenza took over as editor of *California Arts and Architecture,* and by 1943 he had recast the magazine into an open propaganda vehicle for the new architecture.[134] A similar change occurred in architectural photography with the emergence of Julius Shulman as Southern California's dominant interpreter of the new architecture.

The architectural profession in Los Angeles itself was radically changed. A number of the large architectural firms that had dominated the L.A. scene in the '20s and '30s were either gone or were quite small. New names, such as Walter Wurdeman and Welton Becket, Douglas Honnold, and Sumner Spaulding, slowly emerged as the major architectural firms.

Other firms of the '30s became specialists and, thereby, obtained a large percentage of the jobs in one category or another. S. Charles Lee came close to cornering the theatre market, and Norman Marsh, David Smith, and Herbert Powell designed a lion's share of the new public school buildings in the L.A. area. But most L.A. architects ran very small offices and concentrated on residential commissions. Some made a passable living at it; others managed just to get by. All were sustained by a sense of optimism, a belief in man (and particularly the architect), and a belief in technology.

L.A. at the end of the '30s had arrived at one of her golden ages (the others being the end of the '20s and the 1950s). A remarkable series of balances had been achieved between the pressures of population, the economic development of the region, and the potential of what technology and society could achieve. Such points in history are always delicate and short-lived.

NOTES

1. Los Angeles County, Regional Planning Commission, *Master Plan of Highways* (Los Angeles, 1941), 22.

2. Paul Hunter, "Mr. Wright Goes to Los Angeles," *Pencil Points* 21 (March 1940): 34.

3. Oscar Shuch, *The California Scrapbook* (New York, 1869), 204.

4. Robert M. Fogelson, *The Fragmented Metropolis* (Cambridge, 1967), 137-47.

5. Richard Sachse, "Transit: The Movement of People," in George W. Robbins and L. Deming Tilton, *Los Angeles: A Preface to A Master Plan* (Los Angeles, 1941), 101-13.

6. Los Angeles County, Regional Planning Commission, *Master Plan of Highways,* 29.

7. Ralph Hancock, *Fabulous Boulevard* (New York, 1949), 239-306.

8. The Richfield Building was designed by Stiles O. Clements of Morgan, Walls and Clements in 1928; Claud Beelman designed the Columbia and Eastern Outfitters Building in 1929-30.

9. Craig Dale, "Is Main Street Doomed?," *Popular Mechanics* 55 (May 1931): 765-8.

10. Ibid., 768; "Drive-in Markets Help Solve Traffic Problem," *Popular Mechanics* 51 (October 1929): 585.

11. Los Angeles, Department of City Planning, *City Planning in Los Angeles* (Los Angeles, 1964), 23-24; G. Gordon Whitnall, "Tracing the Development of Planning in Los Angeles," in Los Angeles, City Planning Commission, *Annual Report* (Los Angeles, 1929-30); Willard A. Ridings, "A Model for City Planning," *Engineering News Record* 127 (July 17, 1941): 107-8.

12. John D. Weaver, *El Pueblo Grande* (Los Angeles, 1973), 77-78.

13. Grace A. Somerby, "When Los Angeles Was Host to the Olympic Games of 1932," *Historical Society of Southern California Quarterly* 34, no. 2 (June 1952): 125-30.

14. Mel Scott, *Metropolitan Los Angeles: One Community* (Los Angeles, 1949), 37.

15. Margaret Gilbert Mackey, *Cities in the Sun* (Los Angeles, 1938), 164.

16. Scott, *Metropolitan Los Angeles: One Community,* 41.

17. Esther McCoy, "Wilshire Blvd.," *Western Architect and Engineer* 222 (September 1961): 24-51.

18. Ralph D. Cornell, "The Importance of Appearance," in Robbins and Tilton, *Los Angeles: Preface to a Master Plan,* 231.

19. Ibid., 231.

20. Richard J. Neutra, "Homes and Housing," in Robbins and Tilton, *Los Angeles: Preface to a Master Plan,* 191.

21. Mel Scott, *Cities are for People* (Los Angeles, 1942), 67.

22. Ibid., 27.

23. The term "freeway" is to be found in the pages of *California Highways and Public Works,* the official journal of the Department of Public Works of the State of California, Sacramento (1936 and after).

24. S.V. Cortelyou, "Arroyo Seco Parkway Will Include a Six Mile Double Lane Depressed Arterial," *California Highways and Public Works* 14 (August 1936): 25.

25. S.V. Cortelyou, "Cahuenga Freeway Unit Opened," *California Highways and Public Works* 18 (July 1940): 2-24, 17; C.P. Montgomery, "Second Cahuenga Freeway Unit," *California Highways and Public Works* 19 (March 1941): 24-26.

26. G. Gordon Whitnall, *Tracing the Development of Planning in Los Angeles* (Los Angeles, 1930); E.E. East, "Streets: The Circulatory System," in Robbins and Tilton, *Los Angeles: Preface to a Master Plan,* 91-100.

27. "California Pools," *California Arts and Architecture* 57 (April 1940): 32-33.

28. Howard Nelson, "The Spread of an Artificial Landscape over Southern California," in R.W. Durrenberger and P.F. Mason, *Geography of California in Easy Readings* (Los Angeles, 1959), 284-304.

29. Neutra, "Homes and Housing," 189.

30. Clifford M. Zierer, "The Land Use Patterns," in Robbins and Tilton, *Los Angeles: Preface to a Master Plan,* 58.

31. Michael Goodman, "Spirit of Eldorado," *Pencil Points* 22 (May 1941): 291.

32. Zierer, "The Land Use Patterns," 43-59; Scott, *Metropolitan Los Angeles: One Community;* Scott, *American City Planning* (Berkeley, 1969), 204-10; Robert M. Fogelson, *The Fragmented Metropolis* (Cambridge, 1967), 247-76.

33. "Dream City," *Time* 38 (10 November 1941): 45-46; "Now We Plan," *California Arts and Architecture* 57 (November 1941): 21-22.

34. Henry-Russell Hitchcock, "An Eastern Critic Looks at Western Architecture," *California Arts and Architecture* 57 (December 1940): 23.

35. Scott, *Cities are for People,* 46.

36. Gordon Wright, "Food and Functionalism," *California Arts and Architecture* 54 (October 1938): 28, 36.

37. Ibid., 36.

38. Stiles O. Clements, "Thrifty Mart, Los Angeles, California," *Architectural Record* 76 (September 1934): 206; "Owl Drug Store," *Architect and Engineer* 127 (September 1936): 67.

39. "'Drive-in' Bank Opens New Field," *American Builder and Building Age* 60 (February 1938): 52-53. A second drive-in bank, the Farmers and Merchant's Bank, was built later in Long Beach; "Farmers and Merchant's Bank, Long Beach," *Architect and Engineer* 147 (October 1941): 13.

40. Chester H. Liebs, *Main Street Miracle Mile: American Roadside Architecture* (Boston, 1985), 153-7; "Drive-in Theatre, Camden, New Jersey," *Architectural Record* 75 (March 1934): 235; "Drive-in Theatres," *Colliers* 22 (March 1938): 52.

41. S. Charles Lee, "Florence Theatre, Los Angeles," *Architectural Forum* 57 (September 1932): 217-218.

42. Jim Heimann and Rip George (with an introduction by David Gebhard), *California Crazy* (San Francisco, 1980), 11-25. A number of California examples of programmatic architecture are illustrated in J.J.C. Andrews, *The Well-Built Elephant and Other Roadside Attractions* (Boston, 1984).

43. Gordon B. Kaufmann, "Santa Anita Park," *California Arts and Architecture* 47 (February 1935): 24, 25; Burton A. Schutt, "Carl's Sea Air Cafe, Santa Monica," *Architect and Engineer* 139 (October 1939): 22-23.

44. Hitchcock, "An Eastern Critic Looks at Western Architecture," 23.

45. Albert C. Martin and S.A. Marx, "Los Angeles Department Store for the May Department Stores Co.," *Architectural Forum* 72 (May 1940): 353-7; "New Two-Million Dollar Store Building on Wilshire Blvd.," *Southwest Builder and Contractor* 97 (October 20, 1939): 12-13.

46. "New Store Provides for Motorized Patrons," *Architectural Record* 84 (November 1938): 42-47.

47. Albert B. Gardner, "Broadway, Pasadena," *California Arts and Architecture* 58 (February 1941): 26-27.

48. John Stokes Reddon, "Store Building for Sears Roebuck and Co., Los Angeles," *Architectural Forum* 72 (February 1940): 70-76.

49. Ibid., 70.

50. Kaufmann, "Santa Anita Park," 24-25; Stiles O. Clements, "The Hollywood Turf Club, Inglewood," *California Arts and Architecture* 53 (June 1938): 22-23.

51. "Work on Big Racing Plant at Arcadia Now Underway," *Southwest Builder and Contractor* 83 (June 1934): 18-19; "Architectural Treatment of Racing Plant at Arcadia is Pleasing," *Southwest Builder and Contractor* 85 (January 25, 1935): 12-14.

52. "Ice Skating Beneath a Torrid Sun," *Architect and Engineer* 136 (March 1939): 57. Later in 1939, a second year-round, out-of-doors ice skating rink was projected for Lakewood Village in north Long Beach (designed by Wayne D. McAllister); "Lakewood Village Outdoor Ice Rink," *Southwest Builder and Contractor* 94 (December 15, 1939): 28.

53. Lyons Van and Storage Co., Beverly Hills, was designed by Ulysses Floyd Rible, 1941-42; Kem Weber, "Walt Disney Studios," *California Arts and Architecture* 58 (January 1941): 26-27; Walt Disney Studios are First to be Completely Air-Conditioned," *Southwest Builder and Contractor* 95 (April 19, 1940): 12-14, 30.

54. Robert V. Derrah, "The Coca-Cola Plant," *California Arts and Architecture* 50 (November 1936): 43.

55. Robert V. Derrah, "Cross Roads of the World, Hollywood, California," *California Arts and Architecture* 51 (January 1937): 24-25; Robert V. Derrah, "Unique Architectural Treatment of Hollywood Shopping Center," *Southwest Builder and Contractor* 88 (November 1936): 12-13.

56. Edwin Turnbladh, "A Story in a Nutshell," *California Arts and Architecture* 49 (March 1946): 18-19.

57. Gordon B. Kaufmann, "Vultee Aircraft, Inc., Downey, California," *California Arts and Architecture* 58 (May 1941): 32-33, 43; John and Donald B. Parkinson, "Vega Aviation Plant, Burbank, California," *California Arts and Architecture* 58 (March 1941): 34; E.S. Kittrick Co., Inc., "Northrop Aircraft Inc. Plant, Huntington Park," *California Arts and Architecture* 58 (July 1941): 34.

58. Myron Hunt and H.C. Chambers, "Saks Fifth Avenue Store, Beverly Hills," *California Arts and Architecture* 53 (June 1938): 20-21; the I. Magnin Co. Store, Beverly Hills, was illustrated in *Architectural Record* 87 (March 1940): 16.

59. Gordon B. Kaufmann, "Library of the Los Angeles County Medical Association," *California Arts and Architecture* 47 (March 1935): 16; Paul R. Williams, "Music Corp. of America Bldg., Beverly Hills," *Architect and Engineer* 141 (June 1940): 18.

60. "Small Shops with Architectural Distinction," *California Arts and Architecture* 48 (December 1935): 21, 35. Characteristic of these more modest "Colonial-style" retail stores was the group at 6322-32 Wilshire Boulevard, designed in 1936-37 by A.C. Martin; "A Colonial Style Store Building . . . ," *Southwest Builder and Contractor* 89 (June 11, 1927): 11.

61. J.R. Davidson, "Small Shops," *Architectural Record* 66 (October 1929): 355-60.

62. C.W. Short and R. Stanley-Brown, *Public Buildings: Architecture Under the Public Works Administration,* 1933 to 1939 (Washington, 1939), 683, 685.

63. Frederick H. Gutheim, "Seven Years of Public Building," *Magazine of Art* 33 (July 1940): 443.

64. "A Modern City Plans for its Future," *California Arts and Architecture* 57 (November 1940): 22-23.

65. William H. Schuchardt, "The Civic Center," in Robbins and Tilton, *Los Angeles: Preface to a Master Plan,* 239-49.

66. The members of the 1939 Southern California A.I.A. Chapter involved in developing the proposed design for the Civic Center were: Sumner Spaulding, D.C. Allison, and Palmer Sabin; "Progress on Civic Center Plan for Los Angeles is Reported by Architects Group," *Southwest Builder and Contractor* 82 (September 15, 1933): 11; "A Modern City Plans Its Future," *California Arts and Architecture* 57 (November 1940): 22-24. Eventually a number of other L.A. architects contributed to the A.I.A. plan for the Civic Center; these included: John C. Austin, Stiles O. Clements, Ralph C. Flewelling, Earl T. Heitschmidt, Myron Hunt, and William H. Schuchardt; "Architects and Officials Who Developed New Civic Center Plan are Honored," *Southwest Builder and Contractor* 97 (March 21, 1941): 14.

67. Sumner Spaulding, "Los Angeles Civic Center," *Pencil Points* 22 (May 1941): 303.

68. The Long Beach City Hall was, in part, a rebuilding and modernization of an older City Hall, which was damaged by the 1933 earthquake; the transformation of the City Hall into a "modernistic treatment," was by the architect Cecil Schilling; "Rehabilitated Long Beach City Hall in Modernistic Style," *Southwest Builder and Contractor* 84 (December 14, 1934): 10.

69. "Housing Exposition Fulfills Object For Which It Is Sponsored," *Southwest Builder and Contractor* 85 (May 24, 1935): 12-13.

70. "Griffith Park Observatory is Famed Afar; Excites Popular Interest," *Southwest Builder and Contractor* 85 (June 28, 1935): 12-13.

71. "Aqueduct Water Softening Plant to be Imposing Group of Structures," *Southwest Builder and Contractor* 94 (September 13, 1939): 12-14; "Bids are Called for Hayfield Pumping Plant on Colorado Aqueduct," *Southwest Builder and Contractor* 88 (July 24, 1936): 12-13; "Massive Substructure Features Pumping Plants on Colorado Aqueduct," *Southwest Builder and Contractor* 92 (September 16, 1938): 12-15.

72. "Sepulveda Flood Control Dam Unusual Engineering Project," *Southwest Builder and Contractor* 94 (December 1, 1939): 20-22; "Outstanding Features in Construction of Largest Compact Earth Fill Dam," *Southwest Builder and Contractor* 96 (September 1940): 16-18, 21.

73. "Schools," *California Arts and Architecture* 50 (November 1936): 29-35.

74. "Gothic Design for College Buildings at Mount St. Marys," *Southwest Builder and Contractor* 94 (December 15, 1939): 18; "New Edifice for Sanctuary of Our Lady of Guadalupe," *Southwest Builder and Contractor* 94 (December 15, 1939): 20; "Splendid New Edifice for Hollywood Congregation," *Southwest Builder and Contractor* 86 (October 11, 1935): 12-13.

75. "The Los Angeles Union Passenger Terminal," *California Arts and Architecture* 55 (June 1939): 28-29, 40; "Los Angeles Union Passenger Station is Beautiful Architectural Creation," *Southwest Builder and Contractor* 93 (April 28, 1939): 10-13.

76. The terminal was designed by John and Donald B. Parkinson, with Herman Sachs, color consultant and designer, and Tommy Tompson, landscape architect; Paul Hunter, "An Architect's Impressions of New Los Angeles Union Railroad Station," *Southwest Builder and Contractor* 94 (July 14, 1939): 18.

77. Joel L. Hopkins, "Nudes, Locomotives and

Oil Wells," *Westways* 64 (March 1973): 24-29; *The Public Works of Art Project, 14th Region—Southern California,* exhibition catalogue, Los Angeles Museum, Exposition Park, March 1934; Merle Armitage, "Public Works of Art Project," *California Arts and Architecture* 45 (February 1934): 20, 30.

78. Prominent examples of public art in private buildings in downtown Los Angeles, completed before 1931, were in the Stock Exchange (1939-30), the Title Guarantee Building (1930), and the Southern California Edison Building (1930-31).

79. "Siqueiros' Fresco at Chouinard," *California Arts and Architecture* 41 (July-August 1932): 2.

80. Frederick J. Schwankovsky, "A Mural in Search of a Wall," *California Arts and Architecture* 54 (October 1938): 15, 34.

81. Stanton McDonald-Wright's mural was illustrated in *California Arts and Architecture* 48 (September 1935): 9; Grace Clements' murals were illustrated in *California Arts and Architecture* 59 (December 1942): 32-33.

82. The murals in Griffith Observatory were illustrated in *California Arts and Architecture* 47 (March 1935): 11, 12-16; those in the Federal Building were partially illustrated in Works Progress Administration, Writers' Program, *Los Angeles: A Guide to the City and Its Environs* (New York, 1941), illustrations following page 10; and information about *Gastronomy Through the Ages* was presented in *California Arts and Architecture* 47 (March 1935): 6.

83. Walker, Albert R. and Percy A. Eisen, "Sunkist Bldg., Los Angeles," *California Arts and Architecture* 49 (February 1936): 17.

84. William Richards, "State Mutual Loan Association Bldg., Los Angeles," *California Arts and Architecture* 47 (March 1935): 20-21.

85. Gordon B. Kaufmann, "The Los Angeles Times Bldg., Los Angeles," *California Arts and Architecture* 48 (October 1935): 20-23; "Many Unusual Construction Features in Great Newspaper Building," *Southwest Builder and Contractor* 83 (April 13, 1934): 18-19.

86. The photo-mural by Will Connell in the offices of the Columbia Steel Co., Los Angeles, were illustrated in "Columbia Steel Company, Los Angeles, Earl Heitschmidt, Architect," *California Arts and Architecture* 54 (July 1938): 21-32.

87. Harold Wilson's sculpture in front of the Ambassador Hotel was illustrated in *California Arts and Architecture* 53 (March 1938): 7.

88. A report by the Housing Authority of the County of Los Angeles, *A Review of Activities of the Housing Authority of the County of Los Angeles, 1938-43* (Los Angeles, 1943), 45-69 discusses 11 housing projects: Alisos Village, Avalon Gardens, Camelitos Housing Project, Estrada Courts, Lake City Housing Project, William Mead Homes Project, Marville Housing Project, Ramona Gardens, Pico Gardens, Rose Hill Court Housing Project, and Wyvernwood Village. Of the 11, five were completed under the Lanham Act; "Los Angeles Completes Five Lanham Act Projects," *Architect and Engineer* 154 (September 1943): 13-25.

89. "Ramona Gardens," *California Arts and Architecture* 57 (December 1940): 34-35; "Paint Styling Gives Glamour to Buildings In Ramona Gardens Low-Rent Housing Project," *Southwest Builder and Contractor* 97 (February 21, 1941): 8-10; "Alisos Village," *California Arts and Architecture* 59 (October 1942): 38-39.

90. The Harbor Hills Project was illustrated in "Harbor Hills Housing," *California Arts and Architecture* 58 (July 1941): 32.

91. The most significant defense housing projects in the L.A. area were Banning Homes, Channel Heights, Harbor Hills, and Rancho San Pedro in San Pedro; Defense Housing in Long Beach; Normont Terrace and Pueblo del Rio (originally planned as low-cost housing) in Los Angeles; Dana Strand Vil-

173

lage, Wilmington Hall, and Wilmington Annex in Wilmington; and Victory Park in Compton. For Neutra's Channel Heights project, see Elizabeth Mock, ed., *Built in USA, 1932-1944* (New York, 1944), 23, 68-71; Esther McCoy, *Richard Neutra* (New York, 1960), 24-25; Thomas Hines, *Richard Neutra and the Search for Modern Architecture* (New York, 1982), 179-81.

92. The most important of these private projects were Olympic Village, View Park, and the Aetna Housing Project.

93. Wyvernwood was designed by David J. Witmore and Loyall F. Watson; David J. Witmore, "Problems of Planning Large Scale Housing Discussed by Architect," *Southwest Builder and Contractor* 94 (July 14, 1939): 12-13.

94. "Subsistence Homesteads are Planned for Economy and Comfort," *Southwest Builder and Contractor* 84 (November 9, 1934): 26-28; "Rurban Homes Project Near El Monte Now Nearing Completion," *Southwest Builder and Contractor* 86 (August 9, 1935): 12-13.

95. The Aetna Housing Project was designed by W. George Lutzi.

96. Two examples of the private garden apartments of the '30s are Paul R. Williams' Sunset Plaza Apartments, which were illustrated in "Sunset Plaza Apartments, Hollywood," *Architect and Engineer* 129 (June 1939): 36; and "A Hollywood Apartment for John Planje, designed by Milton J. Black," *California Arts and Architecture* 47 (March 1935): 26.

97. R.M. Schindler, "Contemporary House Gaining Favor Local Architect Declares," *Southwest Builder and Contractor* 86 (September 13, 1935): 12-13.

98. William Orr Ludlow, "Modernistic House Probably Never Will be Popular, Architect Declares," *Southwest Builder and Contractor* 86 (July 12, 1935): 24.

99. "Winners are Named in Hundred Year House Competition," *Southwest Builder and Contractor* 84 (November 30, 1934): 9-11.

100. A.B. Laing, "Designing Motion Picture Sets," *Architectural Record* 74 (July 1933): 59-64; Edwin Turnbladh, "When a Room is a Stage," *California Arts and Architecture* 52 (September 1937): 9; "The Influence of Motion Pictures on Interiors," *California Arts and Architecture* 50 (1936): 26; Allen W. Porter, "Hollywood Interiors," *Interiors* 100 (April 1941): 22-28; "Furniture Found In Films," *Sunset* 78 (February 1937): 16; Neutra, "Homes and Housing," 196.

101. David Gebhard and Harriette Von Breton, *Lloyd Wright, Architect* (Santa Barbara, 1971), 22; David Gebhard and Harriette Von Breton, *Kem Weber, The Moderne in Southern California, 1920-1941* (Santa Barbara, 1969), 42, 77, 78; Donald Albrect, *Designing Dreams* (New York, 1986).

102. The picture *What a Widow* was illustrated in *California Arts and Architecture* 39 (April 1931): 40; three sets from the picture *Shall We Dance?* were illustrated in *California Arts and Architecture* 52 (October 1937): 30.

103. Anson B. Cutts, "Homes of Tomorrow in the Movies of Today," *California Arts and Architecture* 54 (November 1938): 22-23.

104. "Successful Transplant," *Sunset* 86 (April 1941): 20-21; the Robert Taylor/Barbara Stanwyck house in San Marino was designed by William D. Holdredge.

105. Advertisement of Pacific Gas Radiator Co., *California Arts and Architecture* 57 (November, 1940): 14.

106. A.E. Hanson, *Rolling Hills, The Early Years* (Rolling Hills, 1978), 75-79.

107. "A New England Village in San Fernando Valley," *Country Life* 74 (September 1938): 54-55.

108. John Chase, *Exterior Decoration: Hollywood's Inside-out Houses* (Los Angeles, 1982), 52-54.

109. Advertising brochure for the West-Side Village Co., *"Get Ready to Live" in West-Side Village* (Los Angeles, 1940).

110. "Large Spanish Style House Planned for Wooded Hillside Site," *Southwest Builder and Contractor* 96 (September 20, 1940): 3.

111. David Gebhard, "The Monterey Tradition: History Re-ordered," *New Mexico Studies in the Fine Arts* 7 (1982): 14-19.

112. "They Make Models for Model Homes" *Sunset* 79 (August 1937): 28.

113. Eloise Roorbach, "A Modern Hacienda on a California Hilltop," *Arts and Decoration* 48 (June 1938): 10-13, 32; Cliff Mays' own house in Mandeville Canyon was illustrated in "The Rancheria of Mr. and Mrs. Cliff May," *California Arts and Architecture* 56 (August 1939): 24.

114. "L'ecole Neutra," *L'Architecture d'Aujourd'hui* 9.1 (June 1938): 37-38.

115. The Sheppard and the Gilks houses were illustrated in *California Arts and Architecture* 47 (January 1935): 23.

116. Williams Lingenbrink, *Park Moderne* (Los Angeles, c. 1932).

117. See illustrations in Paul Laszlo, *Designed in the U.S.A., 1937-1947* (Beverly Hills, 1947).

118. Gebhard and Von Breton, *Kem Weber: The Moderne in Southern California,* 1920-1941, 37-108.

119. J.R. Davidson's Stothart house was illustrated in "Herbert Stothart House, Santa Monica," *California Arts and Architecture* 57 (May 1940): 26-27; his house for Thomas Mann was illustrated in "House for Thomas Mann," *California Arts and Architecture* 59 (December 1942): 36-37.

120. Hitchcock, "An Eastern Critics Look At Western Architecture," 23.

121. The inspiration Ain drew from Schindler, and Modernism in general, can be seen in the Ernest house (Los Angeles, 1937). The William Alexander (Alexander Levy) Halliburton house (Laguna Beach, 1937) is more independent of both Schindler and Neutra; "Reinforced Concrete House for Richard Halliburton, Laguna Beach, California; Alexander Levy, Designer and Builder," *Architect and Engineer* 132 (January 1938): 22.

122. Both Harris and Ain produced several designs bearing the imprint of the Architectural Group for Industry and Commerce; the major figures in this group were R.M. Schindler, Richard J. Neutra, and urban planner Carol Arnovici.

123. *Architectural Record* 92 (November 1942): 49.

124. Gregory Ain, "Design for Post-war Living Competition," *California Arts and Architecture* 60 (August 1943): 27.

125. "Landscape Architects," *Architect and Engineer* 115 (November 1933): 53.

126. "About the Garden Screen," *Sunset* 80 (January 1938): 25.

127. "House Plans Come to Life," *Sunset* 77 (July 1936): 18-19; "Exhibition House Group," *Architectural Forum* 65 (July 1936): 37-46.

128. "Swimming Pools," *Sunset* 78 (April 1937): 26-27.

129. Examples of furniture by Paul R. Williams were illustrated in "Furniture Designed, Executed by Paul Williams of Glendale," *California Arts and Architecture* 50 (October 1936): 7; the "Monterey Furniture" line of Barker Brothers was illustrated in *California Arts and Architecture* 37 (May 1930): 55.

130. "This Month's How-To-Do-It: A Covered-Wagon Garden Seat," *Sunset* 81 (November 1938): 44.

131. Kem Weber, "Two Rooms," *California Arts and Architecture* 54 (July 1938): 10; Gebhard and Von Breton, *Kem Weber, The*

Moderne in Southern California, 1920-1941, 75-100; David Gebhard, "Kem Weber: Moderne Design in California, 1920-1940," *The Journal of Decorative and Propaganda Arts* 2 (Summer/Fall 1986): 20-31.

132. Examples of Paul T. Frankl's furniture were illustrated in *California Arts and Architecture* 54 (July 1938): 16-17; 54 (December 1938): 26-27; 58 (October 1941): 23; 58 (December 1941): 16.

133. Furniture by Hendrick Van Keppel was illustrated in "Modern Furniture by Hendrick Van Keppel," *California Arts and Architecture* 58 (August 1941): 13. For Maria Kipp see Dorothy Bryan, "Maria Kipp—Her Career as a Weaver," *Handweaver and Craftsman* 3, no. 1 (Winter 1951-52): 15-17, 59.

134. For the February 1944 issue, Entenza dropped "California" from the magazine's name, further suggesting that the magazine had fully attached itself to the Modern (i.e., International) Style.

BIBLIOGRAPHY

Andrews, J.J.C. *The Well-Built Elephant and Other Roadside Attractions.* New York: Longdon and Weed, 1984.

Andre, Herb. *John Byers: Domestic Architecture in Southern California, 1919-1960.* M.A. thesis, University of California, Santa Barbara, 1971.

Banham, Reyner. *Los Angeles: The Architecture of Four Ecologies.* London: Penguin, 1971.

Bogardus, Emory Stephen. *Southern California, A Center of Culture.* Los Angeles: University of Southern California Press, 1938.

Bowron, Mrs. Fletcher, ed. *Los Angeles and Its Environs in the Twentieth Century: A Bibliography of a Metropolis.* Los Angeles: Ward Ritchie Press, 1973.

Bradley, Bill. *The Last of the Great Stations.* Los Angeles: Interurban Publications, 1979.

Bricker, David Paul. *Built For Sale: Cliff May and The Low Cost California Ranch House.* M.A. thesis, University of California, Santa Barbara, 1983.

Bricker, Lauren Weiss. *The Residential Architecture of Roland E. Coate.* M.A. thesis, University of California, Santa Barbara, 1982.

Bryant, Lynn. "Edward Huntsman-Trout, Landscape Architect," *Review,* Southern California Chapter, Society of Architectural Historians 2, no. 1 (Winter, 1983): 1-6.

Burdette, Robert J., ed. *Greater Los Angeles and Southern California.* Los Angeles: Lowes Publishing, 1960.

"California Pools." *California Arts and Architecture* 57 (April 1940): 32-33.

Chapman, John L. *Incredible Los Angeles.* New York: Harper and Row, 1967.

Chase, John. *Exterior Decoration: Hollywood's Inside-out Houses.* Los Angeles: Hennessey & Ingalls, 1982.

Clark, Alson. "The California Architecture of Gordon Kaufmann," *Review,* Southern California Chapter, Society of Architectural Historians 1, no. 3 (Summer, 1982): 1-7.

Clark, Alson, Jean Block, Jan Furey Muntz, Robert Judson Clark, Stephanos Polyzoides, Peter de Bretteville, and Robert Winter. *Myron Hunt, 1868-1952: The Search for a Regional Architecture.* Santa Monica: Hennessey & Ingalls, 1984.

Clark, Robert Judson and Thomas S. Hines. *Los Angeles Transfer: Architecture in Southern California 1880-1980.* Los Angeles: University of California, Los Angeles, William Andrews Clark Library, 1983.

Cleland, Robert Glass and Osgood Hardy. *March of Industry.* Los Angeles: Powell, 1929.

Crump, Spencer. *Ride the Big Red Cars.* Los Angeles: Crest Publications, 1962.

Cutts, Anson B. "Radio City, California Style." *California Arts and Architecture* 55 (January 1939): 28.

Feldman, Eddy S. *The Art of Street Lighting in Los Angeles.* Los Angeles: Dawson's Book Shop, 1972.

Fogelson, Robert M. *The Fragmented Metropolis: Los Angeles 1850-1930.* Cambridge: Harvard University Press, 1967.

Frankl, Paul T. "Modern Will Live." *California Arts and Architecture* 53 (March 1938): 17-19.

Frankl, Paul T. *Space for Living.* New York: Doubleday, Doran, 1938.

Gebhard, David. *George Washington Smith.* Santa Barbara: University of California, Santa Barbara, Art Galleries, 1964.

Gebhard, David. *The International Style in Southern California.* Riverside: University of California, Riverside, University Art Gallery, 1987.

Gebhard, David. "Kem Weber: Modern Design in California, 1920-1940," *The Journal of Decorative and Propaganda Arts* 2 (Summer/Fall 1986): 20-31.

Gebhard, David. "L.A.—The Stuccoed Box." *Art in America* 58 (May-June 1970): 130-133.

Gebhard, David. "The Monterey Tradition: History Re-ordered," *New Mexico Studies in the Fine Arts* 7 (1982): 14-19.

Gebhard, David (with a foreword by Henry-Russell Hitchcock). *Schindler.* New York: Viking, 1972.

Gebhard, David. "The Spanish Colonial Revival in Southern California." *Journal of the Society of Architectural Historians* 26 (May 1967): 131-147.

Gebhard, David and Harriette Von Breton. *1868-1968 Architecture in California.* Santa Barbara: University of California, Santa Barbara, Art Galleries, 1968.

Gebhard, David and Harriette Von Breton. *Kem Weber: The Moderne in Southern California, 1920-1941.* Santa Barbara: University of California, Santa Barbara, Art Galleries, 1969.

Gebhard, David and Harriette Von Breton. *Lloyd Wright, Architect.* Santa Barbara: University of California, Santa Barbara, Art Galleries, 1971.

Gebhard, David, Harriette Von Breton, and Lauren Weiss Bricker. *The Architecture of*

Gregory Ain: The Play between the Rational and High Art. Santa Barbara: University of California, Santa Barbara, University Art Museum, 1980.

Gebhard, David and Robert Winter. *Architecture in Southern California.* Los Angeles: Los Angeles County Museum of Art, 1965.

Gebhard, David and Robert Winter. *Architecture in Los Angeles.* Salt Lake City: Peregrine Smith Books, 1985.

Gill, Brendan. *The Dream Come True: The Great Houses of Los Angeles.* New York: Lippincott and Crowell, 1980.

Gleye, Paul. *The Architecture of Los Angeles.* Los Angeles: Rosebud Books, 1981.

Hamlin, Talbot F. "What Makes it American: Architecture in the Southwest and West." *Pencil Points* 20 (December 1939): 762-776.

Hancock, Ralph. *Fabulous Boulevard.* New York: Funk & Wagnalls, 1949.

Hanson, A.E. *Rolling Hills: The Early Years.* Rolling Hills: City of Rolling Hills, 1978.

Hanson, Earl and Paul Beckett. *Los Angeles: Its People and Its Homes.* Los Angeles: Haynes Foundation, 1944.

Heimann, Jim and Rip George (with an introduction by David Gebhard). *California Crazy.* San Francisco: Chronicle Books, 1980.

Henstell, Bruce. *Los Angeles: An Illustrated History.* New York: Alfred A. Knopf, 1980.

Hines, Thomas S. *Richard Neutra and the Search for Modern Architecture.* New York: Oxford University Press, 1982.

Hitchcock, Henry-Russell. "An Eastern Critic Looks at Western Architecture." *California Arts and Architecture* 57 (December 1940): 21-23, 40.

"Hollywood Tackles the Parking Problem." *Architectural Record* 88 (December 1940): 45-48.

Hunter, Paul Robinson and Walter L. Reichardt, eds. *Residential Architecture in Southern Califor-*

nia. Los Angeles: American Institute of Architects, Southern California Chapter, 1939.

Kaplan, Sam Hall. *L.A. Lost and Found.* New York: Crown, 1987.

Knight, Arthur and Eliot Elisofon. *The Hollywood Style.* New York: MacMillan, 1969.

Laszlo, Paul. *Designed in the U.S.A., 1937-1947.* Beverly Hills: Paul Laszlo, 1947.

Layne, Gregg. *Books of the Los Angeles District.* Los Angeles: Dawson's Book Shop, 1950.

Liebs, Chester A. *Main Street Miracle Mile: American Roadside Architecture.* Boston: Little, Brown, 1985.

Lingenbrink, William. *Modernistic Architecture.* Los Angeles: privately published, c. 1932.

Lockwood, Charles. *Dream Palaces.* New York: Viking, 1981.

Lockwood, Charles. *The Guide to Hollywood and Beverly Hills.* New York: Crown, 1984.

Los Angeles. City Planning Commission. *Accomplishments.* Los Angeles, editions of 1941, 1942, 1943.

Los Angeles. Department of City Planning. *City Planning in Los Angeles: A History.* Los Angeles, 1964.

Los Angeles County. Housing Authority. *A Decent Home . . . An American Right.* Los Angeles, 1944.

Los Angeles County. Regional Planning Commission. *Annual Report, 1940.* Los Angeles, 1941.

Los Angeles County. Regional Planning Commission. *Annual Report, 1941.* Los Angeles, 1942.

Los Angeles County. Regional Planning Commission. *Changes in Population Census Tracts in Los Angeles County, 1930-1940.* Los Angeles, 1940.

Los Angeles County. Regional Planning Commission. *Master Plan of Highways.* Los Angeles, 1941.

Los Angeles County. Regional Planning Commission. *Master Plan of Land Use—Inventory and Classification.* Los Angeles, 1941.

Los Angeles County. Regional Planning Commission, *A Comprehensive Report on the Master Plan of Highways for Los Angeles County.* Los Angeles, 1941.

Mackey, Margaret Gilbert. *Los Angeles, Proper and Improper.* Los Angeles: Goodwin Press, 1938.

Mayo, Morrow. *Los Angeles.* New York: Knopf, 1933.

McCoy, Esther. *Five California Architects.* New York: Reinhold, 1960.

McCoy, Esther. *Irving Gill 1870-1936.* Los Angeles: Los Angeles County Museum of Art, 1958.

McCoy, Esther. *Richard Neutra.* New York: Braziller, 1960.

McCoy, Esther. "Roots of California Contemporary Architecture." *Arts and Architecture* 73 (October 1956): 14-17.

McCoy, Esther. *The Second Generation.* Salt Lake City: Peregrine Smith, 1984.

McCoy, Esther. "Wilshire Blvd." *Western Architect and Engineer* 222, no. 3 (September 1961): 24-51.

McWilliams, Carey. *Southern California Country.* 1946. Reprint, Salt Lake City: Peregrine Smith, 1973.

Moore, Charles W., Peter Becker, and Regula Campbell. *The City Observed: Los Angeles—A Guide to Architecture and Landscape.* New York: Vintage, 1984.

Nadeau, Remi. *Los Angeles: From Mission to Modern City.* New York: Longmans, Green, 1960.

Neff, Wallace. *Architecture in Southern California.* Chicago: Rand McNally, 1964.

Neff, Wallace, Jr. and Alson Clark (with a forward by David Gebhard). *Wallace Neff Architect* of California's Golden Age. Santa Barbara: Capra Press, 1986.

Nelson, Howard. "The Spread of an Artificial Landscape over Southern California." In R.W. Durrenberger and P.F. Mason, Geography of California in Essays and Readings, 284-304. Los Angeles: Brewster Publications, 1959.

Neutra, Richard. Life and Shape. New York: Appleton, Century-Crofts, 1962.

New Deal Art in California. Santa Clara: University of Santa Clara, de Saisset Art Gallery and Museum, 1976.

O'Connor, Ben H. "Super Markets," Architectural Record 84 (October 1941): 72-73.

Pildas, Ave. Art Deco Los Angeles. New York: Harper and Row, 1977.

Polyzoides, Stephanos, Roger Sherwood, and James Tice. Courtyard Housing in Los Angeles. Los Angeles and Berkeley: University of California Press, 1982.

Powdermaker, Hortense. Hollywood, the Dream Factory. London: Secker & Warburg, 1951.

Powell, Lawrence Clark. Land of Fiction. Los Angeles: Dawson's Book Shop, 1952.

Rand, Christopher. Los Angeles, The Ultimate City. New York: Oxford University Press, 1967.

Regan, Michael. Mansions of Los Angeles. Los Angeles: Regan Publishing, 1966.

Regan, Michael. Mansions of Beverly Hills. Los Angeles: Regan Publishing, 1966.

Ridings, Willard A. "A Model for City Planning," Engineering News Record 127 (July 17, 1941): 107-108.

Robbins, George W. and L. Deming Tilton, eds. Los Angeles: Preface to a Master Plan. Los Angeles: Pacific Southwest Academy, 1941.

Robinson, W.W. Los Angeles: A Profile. Norman: University of Oklahoma Press, 1968.

Robinson, W.W. Panorama: A Picture-history of Southern California. Los Angeles: Title Insurance and Trust Co., 1953.

Rosten, Leo C. Hollywood: The Movie Colony, The Movies, The Movie Makers. New York: Harcourt Brace, 1941.

Schindler, Pauline (guest editor). "Special Issue Devoted to Modern Architecture in Southern California." California Arts and Architecture 47 (January 1935).

Scott, Mel. Cities are for People. Los Angeles: Pacific Southwest Academy (Publication 21), 1942.

Scott, Mel. Metropolitan Los Angeles: One Community. Los Angeles: Haynes Foundation, 1949.

"Taxpayers from Los Angeles." Architectural Forum 68 (March 1938): 263-265.

Torrance, Bruce. Hollywood: The First 100 Years. Hollywood: Hollywood Chamber of Commerce and Fiske Enterprise, 1979.

Tracy, Robert Howard. John Parkinson and the City Beautiful Movement in Downtown Los Angeles. Ph.D. thesis, University of California, Los Angeles, 1982.

Weaver, John D. El Pueblo Grande. Los Angeles: Ward Ritchie Press, 1973.

Whitnall, Gordon. "Tracing the Development of Planning in Los Angeles," Annual Report. Los Angeles: City Planning Commission, 1930.

Wilson, Richard Guy. "Machine-Age Iconography in the American West," Pacific Historical Review 54, no. 4 (November 1985): 463-493.

Woollett, William (with an introduction by David Gebhard). Hoover Dam: Drawings, Etchings, Lithographs 1931-1933. Santa Monica: Hennessey & Ingalls, 1986.

Winter, Robert. *Myron Hunt at Occidental College.* Los Angeles: Occidental College, 1986.

Workman, Boyle. *The City that Grew, 1840-1936.* Los Angeles: Southland Publishing, 1935.

"Work of Some Contemporary Los Angeles Architects." *Pencil Points* 22 (May 1941): 306-333.

Works Progress Administration. Writers' Program. *Los Angeles: A Guide to the City and Its Environs.* New York: Hastings House, 1941.

Wright, J. Gordon. "Food and Functionalism." *California Arts and Architecture* 54 (October 1938): 28, 36.

PHOTOGRAPHIC CREDITS

Robert E. Alexander: 115, 116

Architect and Engineer: 53, 60, 81, 102, 103, 137

Architectural Forum: 52, 135, 136, 189

Architectural Record: 48, 49, 50, 191

Authors: 31, 37, 39, 43, 51, 55, 58, 59, 61, 64, 65, 68, 69, 75, 83, 84, 85, 93, 97, 98, 101, 105, 107, 109, 110, 112, 113, 119, 120, 123, 124, 126, 129, 133, 134, 138, 139, 156, 157, 160, 162, 168, 169, 170, 194, 203, 207, 208, 209, 212, 219

Miles Berne:* 211

State of California, Department of Transportation (CALTRANS): 24, 25

California Arts and Architecture (Arts and Architecture): 71, 72, 73, 96, 111, 204

Fred R. Dapprich:* 149

First Federal of Hollywood (The Bruce Torrence Historical Collection): 2, 6, 8, 13, 14, 15, 22, 34, 35, 36, 40, 41, 57, 74, 79, 82, 95, 106

George Haight:* 42, 143

Los Angeles County, Regional Planning Commission, *Master Plan of Highways,* 1941: 23, 26

Los Angeles County Museum of Natural History (History Division): 1, 4, 5, 7, 9, 10, 11, 12, 17, 18, 27, 28, 29, 30, 32, 33, 46, 47, 56, 70, 94, 99

Luckhaus Studios: 104, 125, 184

Cliff May: 165, 166

Maynard Parker: 54, 210

Marvin Rand: 67, 196

George W. Robbins and L. Deming Tilton, *Los Angeles: Preface to a Master Plan,* 1941: 21

George Vernon Russell: 80

Mel Scott, *Cities Are For People,* 1942: 19, 20, 92, 100

Julius Shulman: 127, 128, 187, 188, 190, 198, 199, 200, 201, 202, 205

Southwest Builder and Contractor: 62, 63, 86, 87, 88, 91, 108, 114, 117, 118, 122, 130, 131, 132, 154, 158, 159

Sunset: 221

University of California, Los Angeles (Special Collections): 3

University of California, Santa Barbara, Art Galleries (Architectural Drawing Collection): 38, 44, 45, 66, 76, 77, 78, 89, 90, 140, 141, 142, 144, 145, 146, 147, 148, 150, 151, 152, 153, 155, 161, 163, 164, 167, 171, 172, 173, 174, 175, 176, 177, 178, 179, 180, 181, 182, 183, 185, 186, 192, 193, 206, 220, 222, 223, 224, 225

W.P. Woodcock:* 195, 197

Lloyd Wright: 121, 213, 214, 215, 216, 217, 218

*From the University of California, Santa Barbara, University Art Museum, Architectural Drawing Collection

INDEX